Praise for Joel Wolfe a

"I love to find parenting books that inspire both the heart and the head in equal measure. *Courage in Chaos* delivers in spades. Joel Wolfe has something special on her hands with this one!"

—Dr. Kevin Leman, author of *Making Children Mind without Losing Yours* and *The Birth Order Book*

"In this courageous conduit out of chaos, Joel Wolfe provides the modern family with a road map for raising incredible children. *Courage in Chaos* is not only a compelling read but also a vital reference guide that purposeful parents will always keep readily at hand. It is quite clear and enormously reassuring that this book wasn't birthed in remote academic theory but springs from loving, practical parenting consistently applied. You will quickly come to regard it as one of your most crucial allies in the sometimes scary, always challenging, but supremely satisfying job of being a parent."

—Rabbi Daniel Lapin, author of *Thou Shall Prosper* and President of the American Alliance of Jews and Christians

"We love Joel Wolfe's new book, *Courage in Chaos*. It's brilliant, easy to read, and one that you'll return to over and over again for advice. You'll enjoy her real-life examples and solutions discovered through her own experiences, her extensive study of scholarly works, and Scripture on the subject. She's real and holds nothing back from the reader, sharing her own successes and failures openly and honestly. Her book will give you a strong foundation on which to develop children who become strong, responsible adults who are able to wisely navigate life while caring for others, developing healthy relationships, and becoming successful in their life's work and God-given destiny. You'll want to purchase a copy not only for yourself but for others as well."

—Brian Simmons, lead translator of *The Passion Translation*

"*Courage in Chaos* is a delight to read and a highly practical guide to rearing children into healthy, creative young adults. Joel Wolfe is a relentless student of life who shares her wealth of experience and wisdom, distilled into uncomplicated strategies. This isn't simply theory but is tried-and-true wisdom. It is full of fun and totally down-to-earth stories of true adventures, embarassments, and challenges of bringing up four, very much alive, young individuals. There is hope in these pages for any father or mother who needs some easy-to-grasp wisdom for their journey. If you are a parent or grandparent, this book will help you!"

—Charles Stock, Senior Pastor at Life Center Ministries

"With today's ever-changing lifestyles and the fluctuating structure of family, it is so important that we learn God's way of parenting. I believe that *Courage in Chaos* by Joel Wolfe is a great tool for all parents to keep the hedge of God surrounding our homes. Let's work together to raise our families God's way!"

—Linda Sharkey, Senior Pastor at Spokane Christian Center

"Joel Wolfe's book, *Courage in Chaos,* is a delightful read, filled with fantastic parenting advice and adventures, forged in the furnace of personal experience with her own amazing family. This book is not a theoretical treatise on raising children. It's a fun journey through the ups, downs, ins, and outs of the Wolfe family. Joel chronicles her relentless pursuit of putting into practice what really works to raise kids into emotionally healthy, productive adults in this incredibly well-researched, footnoted book. I can attest to her success because I personally know her amazing adult children. I can confidently encourage any parent at any stage of parenting to gain critical wisdom and insight for raising a family by reading *Courage in Chaos!*"

—Michael Proctor, Senior Leader at the Barn, Elisha's Request Ministries

COURAGE
in CHAOS

STRENGTH AND HOPE FOR YOUR ADVENTURES IN PARENTING

by
Joel Wolfe

RESTORED LIFE PRESS

Copyright © 2018 by Joel Wolfe. All rights reserved.

This book may not be reproduced or transmitted, by any form or in any means, without prior written approval from the publisher.

Cover design by Alicia Bilton. Book layout by Byron Leavitt. Editing services provided by the Scribe Source. Book set in Adobe Caslon Pro. The fonts used on the cover and for chapter headings were Aileron, Comic Panels, and Skinny Marker.

Scriptures marked New American Standard Bible or NASB are taken from the NEW AMERICAN STANDARD BIBLE®, Copyright © 1960, 1962, 1963, 1968, 1971, 1972, 1973, 1975, 1977, 1995 by the Lockman Foundation. Used by permission. www.Lockman.org

Scriptures marked New International Version or NIV are taken from THE HOLY BIBLE, NEW INTERNATIONAL VERSION®, NIV® Copyright © 1973, 1978, 1984, 2011 by Biblica, Inc.® Used by permission. All rights reserved worldwide.

Scripture quotations marked New Living Translation or NLT are taken from the *Holy Bible*, New Living Translation, copyright © 1996, 2004, 2015 by Tyndale House Foundation. Used by permission of Tyndale House Publishers, Inc., Carol Stream, Illinois 60188. All rights reserved.

Inquiries can be addressed to:
Restored Life Press
office@newhcc.com

Published by Restored Life Press. Learn more about Restored Life at http://www.restoredlifepress.com.

ISBN-13 (Print): 978-1-947088-00-9
ISBN-13 (eBook): 978-1-947088-01-6

I dedicate this book first of all to my Lord and Savior, Jesus Christ.

Secondly, I dedicate it to my forever friend, encourager, and loving husband, Dwain Wolfe, as well as my personal favorites, Jasmine, Caleb, Austin, and Solomon Sterling. If it weren't for all of you, I would have nothing to write.

Finally, I would like to honor and thank my mother, Phyllis Robertson, who raised me to believe for great things and filled my heart and soul with love and wisdom. I have taken what you taught me and built upon it. You are my hero. I pray this book stands as a testament of God's wisdom for generations to come.

TABLE OF CONTENTS

CHAPTER ONE

LIFE IN THE WOLFE DEN

Many moons ago, the Wolfes birthed their first cub.

A lot has happened since then.

Dwain and I married when I was 19 and he was 24, and five years later, we had our first Wolfe cub. My husband and I were young and starry-eyed. We were not going to make the same mistakes that countless others had made, and our children would rise higher than all others on account of our amazing parenting skills.

The next five years brought two more cubs and a brand-new church that we founded and still copastor today. Cub Number Four came a little later, just in case things weren't exciting enough.

Busy and exciting was okay by us, though. My husband

and I are outgoing, can-do, adventuresome folks who are a little on the loud side. More of the "fire, ready, aim" type than the contemplative, planner type. And we produced four Wolfe cubs that were uncannily like their parents. The exponential effect was that on a good day, life in our family was a bit noisy; on a normal day, it was a bit chaotic; and on particular days, it was *very* loud and *very* chaotic. It was in this arena that we attempted to bring forth those "amazing parenting skills."

From Starry-Eyed Parenting to Harsh Reality

We were full of ideals and ready to change the world. We just knew that the Wolfe Pack was going to be different from all other families. Our cubs were going to love us and thank us for our amazing parenting skills, and after meaningful, momentary explanations, they would see things from our perspective and, therefore, cooperate on all levels from heartfelt understanding. Our children would become prodigy teens with the utmost respect and reverence for their parents. Our young would not taste of the addictions and temptations so common to sixteen-year-olds; instead, they were going to come home and participate in our family worship nights.

Looking back, we are sure we were tricked. It was so easy to get that little bun in the oven, quite another thing to get it out. And it was still quite another to get each one flying solo in the real world.

Newborns are so cute and perfect and (somewhat) quiet at first. As parents, we direct their entire lives, from what type of diaper they will sport to who will hold them to what type of baby food they will ingest. We pick their haircuts, their playdates, and their bedtimes. But somewhere along the line, the fact that they are completely separate individuals with a sovereign free will begins to emerge. They begin to have opinions that are exactly the opposite of ours. And then we find ourselves in the same spot as our parents did with us. The epic, "Wait—what?" comes when they exert that free will and there we stand, tempted to react the same way parents have for many years and sputter, "Because I'm the mom, that's why!" At this point, we all cry out for help as we find that we do not have all the answers and that all this could go very wrong, very fast.

That's exactly what happened at the Wolfe house. Just when Dwain and I thought our kids were going to be different, we realized they weren't. They came with the same inner stuffing as all those that have gone before. Our two-year-olds pitched fits, wouldn't eat, and *had* to dress themselves. (I had nothing to do with the cowboy boots-and-shorts combo!) One of my kindergarteners was so embarrassed that I came in to class to help that he refused to look at me the entire time. My junior high daughter was mortified that as I stood in a circle meeting her new friends, I exclaimed, "Oh my, I knew you when you were a baby! Don't worry, I never changed your diaper!" I thought it was endearing; she didn't talk to me for a week.

Over the next two decades, we had fights, yelling, three broken legs, fifteen dead pets, eighty (yes, eighty) lost teeth, multiple sets of stitches, homemade things that went boom, police at the door, a pickup from juvenile hall (unrelated to explosives), seven car wrecks in five years by three beginning drivers (the fourth cub then had three more accidents within his first year of driving), six surgeries, and numerous trips to the hospital. We have had the overachieving, 4.12-GPA graduate and the one in remedial reading. We have had the "I am not so sure I believe in God" conversations, the "Why can't I drink?" conversations, and the "But marijuana isn't addictive" conversations. And then there were the "If you choose that, you will need to find another place to live" conversations. I'm still not sure if that was the right approach, but it seemed to work, and one of them actually thanked me for that stance just the other day.

Our crazy, chaotic and often overwhelming journey has NOT been boring.

Before we get much further, I should introduce you to the Wolfe Pack. Jasmine is our oldest, a typical firstborn female—overachiever, controller, political science major, and overall amazing getter-done list-lady type. Caleb, born two and a half years later, is the entertainment epicenter of the family, full of fun yet smart enough to become a chemical engineer—as well as Jasmine's ultimate annoyance. Austin, who emerged after another two and a half years, is an incredibly talented, easygoing, peace-brokering, creative young man who is now a mechanical engineer. Solomon Sterling, the caboose, was a bit of a shock, arriving a full five years later. Those shock waves continue to reverberate. I wouldn't trade him for the world, but truth be known, had he been first, he just might have been an only child! Everything I knew and held dear in parenting was severely tested. We were left holding what really counted in parenting as the unimportant things went down the drain. Nicknamed the SS Destroyer, there wasn't much left untouched in his wake.

Despite all the uncertainty these four brought us, I can honestly say we made it! We now have three gainfully employed college graduates with a fourth on his way. All four are living lives dedicated to Christ. All four are successful, independent, financially responsible individuals. At this moment, two are married and the circle of life has begun again with our first grandson. Yet I remember very clearly the agony and fear as we parented to our best abilities and then had to sit back and watch our children make their own choices. I get it.

I had never considered myself some kind of parenting guru. I was just a mom and a pastor who started sharing with others what worked—and didn't work—in our house. What began as casual conversations with moms and dads in the church foyer became Wednesday-night parenting classes, which later became two-day seminars that we opened to the community. And now I get to share with you.

My goal for this book is not to give you a technical or psychological exposé on the deeper concepts of parent-child relationships. Instead, it's going to be a "Let's get *real*" book. I am not a licensed counselor, nor do I have a PhD, but I am someone who can give you courage in your chaos, indomitable hope that you can win, and real-time wisdom to get you over the finish line. I plan to share with you what made the difference in the Wolfe home and how we made it work in practical, down-to-earth ways. I hope my stories will give you courage to parent with a smile on your face and my ideas will give you wisdom that will inspire creativity.

In the next chapter, I'll share with you the fundamentals that were beacons of guiding light in the Wolfe family during very dark times. It's the difficult moments with your children that help you begin to consider which things really matter in parenting and which things, while good ideas, aren't worth shedding blood over. I'll show you how we took those nonnegotiable fundamentals—our core parenting beliefs, so to speak—and used them to engage with our children in certain ways. I'll then take you through a series of chapters that look at practical ways to run your household and family that will instill work ethic, truth, respect, and other character traits that will stand the test of time.

My encouragement for you is to take the principles you learn here and apply them in your unique way. My hope is to give you a strong basic foundation on which you can build your own systems and create the best little family you can, one that's uniquely yours with fun history, traditions, and memories.

Wisdom You Can Make Your Own

I can recall a very pivotal day in my parenting journey, about sixteen months after the birth of Wolfe Cub Number One (the essence of human perfection herself). I found myself in our brown Astro van driving home from the grocery store. Jasmine was in her car seat in the front passenger seat (perfectly legal at the time), and she was fit to be tied. She was throwing what I considered to be her first bona fide stubborn, angry, for-no-apparent-reason fit. As we drove home, I started sweating profusely as I circled through anger, fear, frustration, agony, depression, and the sentiments of "What am I supposed to do?" "I'm a terrible parent," "You're getting a spanking," "Please, oh please just be good," "She is going to choose to be on drugs and everything else," and a few other good thoughts. By the time we arrived home, we were both a mess. I carried her in the house and set her on the couch (a bit more firmly than usual) and proceeded to lecture her on the need for obedience and self-control. When it was apparent that victory was *not* at hand, I went in the kitchen, hoping to find the answers there. The sink full of dirty dishes had nothing to say. I knew I was in trouble. I needed a plan. I needed a strategy. I needed to win. Thus began my search for parenting wisdom.

Unfortunately, or maybe fortunately, when my husband and I first began our journey with the cubs, the internet was not invented yet, so all the blogs and crazy, confusing messages that bombard today's parents were not available. Instead, we had videos! We'd bring out the VCR cart at church and together with our congregation learn about first-time obedience, respect, putting shopping carts back in the stalls, and creating a family culture. We learned so much, and our kids all benefitted from the teaching we sat under. But I also remember feeling very incapable of completely fulfilling all the methods these parenting experts were prescribing. Being the pastor's family, the pressure was real. Though each approach was full of great wisdom, Dwain, our kids, and I were not PhD-textbook perfect.

I believe that though there are basic parenting fundamentals that are true across the board, no two kids are alike, so the approach needs to be a bit more tailor-made for each family. My husband and I did our best to take the principles we learned and make them work for the Wolfe Pack. The case could be made that if I had followed the experts' advice more closely, I would have had better results with the Wolfe cubs. Maybe so. We did as much as our personal strength and growth would allow us to do while at the same time making allowance for our different personalities.

TOP TIP #1

Parenting is as much about the maturation of the parent as about the growth of the child.

I have lived long enough to know that you really don't have to know everything. You only must surround yourself with those who do. So, I didn't stop my parenting education with the church videos. Throughout the years, I have made it a priority to surround myself with the best parenting experts I could find. Unfortunately, they weren't available for coffee, so I settled for their thoughts in written form. I have read and continue to read every parenting book I can find. In addition to my own ideas, the book you now hold is filled with things I learned from the experts—quotes and tidbits from the likes of Dr. James Dobson, Dr. Kevin Leman, Dr. Charles Fay, Jim Fay, and Dr. John Gottman. I would encourage you to not stop with this parenting book but to read everything you can get your hands on. I've included a recommended reading list at the end of this book to get you started.

As you take these concepts and do your best to make them work for you, there is something of great importance that I want you to take into consideration. Parenting is going to challenge you as a human being. I believe parenting is primarily for the maturation of us as parents and, subsequently, for the benefit of the child. You are going to have to grow in love, self-control, self-discipline, and character if you want to be a great parent. This isn't an easy task, but if you are up for it, you will set yourself up for wonderful, lasting relationships with your adult children. They will long to be like you and with you as you yourself have matured into someone they can respect and love.

You stand in such an amazing place. The mere fact that you are searching for wisdom by reading this book indicates you are incredible. I know your children are full of God-given potential. Let's take that first step from chaos to victory by solidifying the basics of parenting in your heart and mind.

Let's make these fleeting years be the best years of both your life and theirs!

CHAPTER TWO

THE TERMS OF ENGAGEMENT

Picture this: I'm standing in the kitchen one morning with a certain Wolfe cub who is about three years old. I am a rational, mature adult with perfectly sensible requests: "You may not color on my walls *or* on your brother with marker! Now, please give me the marker, and let's clean up this mess." The Wolfe cub, a third my size and a fourth my weight, stares up at me, says, "*No!*" and runs away. This is not the first defiance of the day. Oh no, it's more like the tenth—and it is only 9:00 a.m.!

At this point, I am faced with a decision: Do I remain calm, or do I chase the toddler down and wrestle the child into submission with a loud and slightly desperate voice?

I am beginning to question both my status as a rational, mature adult and my ability to win with this mighty foe. I also question the reason I birthed this child in the first place. At this point, a win is surviving the day without any criminal activity or losing my sanity. I begin to plot the exit strategy: "Only fifteen more years . . ." I also begin to compromise: "Okay, okay, so no child prodigy here. If I can get this child to eighteen with all four appendages intact and novice skills with macaroni and cheese, I will have won!" All this child really needs to live independently is a set of wheels (maybe a skateboard or possibly a bicycle), a change of underwear, and a toothbrush, right?

Our first reaction to these little buggers might be to lower ourselves to their level and join in the fray. Sarcasm, threats, yelling, and frustration are easy default settings. Or maybe you are the patient parent, quietly responding to their misbehaviors with calm and lovely words. While I awoke every morning with fresh commitment to this approach, it seemed that given enough time, my niceness would eventually turn toward frustration. In my failures, I learned that simply willing yourself to be a perfect parent doesn't produce good results. Instead, if we can latch onto better, more realistic core parenting truths, grounding our thoughts and acting instead of reacting, we can relocate that reasonable, mature adult who parents for the win!

To return to or remain the reasonable, mature, and, might I add, victorious parent, we need to change our terms of engagement. Your terms of engagement, or rules of parenting, are really your approach or posture. It's first how you think and then how you respond in the moment. Terms of engagement are quite literally the rules that people must follow when they deal with each other. The problem with parenting is that rule following is usually a very one-sided affair. We the parents are aware of the rules of life and relationships, and our sweet little people are generally unaware or nonconforming to these rules. Whichever the case may be, it's our job to turn our little renegades into rule followers.

To do this, we must be the ones who set the terms of engagement. I've found there are four fundamental mind-sets that will help you engage your child successfully, whether toddler or teen. You can base your approach to nearly any challenge on these terms of engagement. These four mind-sets are (1) to understand your ultimate parenting goals, (2) to never break a sweat, (3) to relate to your child with empathy instead of frustration, and (4) to establish healthy boundaries for your children. I believe these four elements will be game changers for you and help you turn things around in your home.

Keep the Ultimate Goals in Mind

As life unfolds with these amazingly smart and industrious littles, it's easy to see your lofty parental aspirations vaporize. This is more normal than you realize. The real question is, What will you do now? I want to encourage you to take those lofty, unrealistic dreams of parenting and set them aside for the better.

After three somewhat-successful toddlerhoods, we had our sweet little caboose. Since he was God's version of a surprise, I figured I had the privilege of putting in a few requests on this one during my pregnancy. I prayed for a very *calm, quiet* girl who looked like me and acted more like her dad (happy hearted and easygoing). I ended up with a *boy* who looked *and* acted like me! I guess one out of three isn't too bad. As I said earlier, he was the one who caused us to strip away the parenting frills and left us standing strong on the nonnegotiables.

When I say "frills," I am referring to those things that, though good, aren't worth dying for. For example, it is very important for me to feed my children healthy food. Wolfe Cub Number Four took it upon himself to give his last drops of blood to never eat breakfast or anything green, be it ever so microscopic, with the

TOP TIP #2

It's important to determine your parenting nonnegotiables and stick with them, while letting less vital things go.

exception of dill pickles. Either we were going to cross swords until one of us was no more or pickles would be the new main course. I'm glad to say we all lived, and by the end of teenage life, he now eats a moderately well-rounded diet. Judge me if you must, but in reality, it takes wisdom to decide what are the nonnegotiables and what aren't.

The first nonnegotiable fundamental mind-set in parenting is to always be mindful of the *ultimate* goals. Not just any goals, but the ones that really, truly matter. That's the only way to know that you have succeeded! We all have goals for our children: be the star of the team, go to bed at a reasonable hour without a fight, get all As in school. These are great, but there are more important goals that need to drive your thought process as you engage your children. These are the goals that at the end of the day, whether they become Olympic champions or valedictorians or neither, you will have succeeded.

I believe that the ultimate goals of parenting are to raise adult children *who love well in their life's relationships* and *who succeed in their life's work*. These two areas are ultimately the most important things in life. Grounding your parenting mind-set on these two things will keep you focused on the right things.

Notice I didn't say to raise adult children who are happy or to raise adult children who have more things than we did. Happiness and things are both by-products of the real issues in life and must be found by each of us individually. I can't supply them for my children; they must produce their own happiness and build their own pile of things. If they don't do this for themselves, they will not have completed the work of maturation. We can't do it for them. It must be their own journey.

First, our children must navigate relationships well by having the ability to love others with selfless empathy, care, and wisdom. Their future marriages and families depend on them grasping the key concepts of covenant relationships—relationships in which loving confrontation, repentance, selflessness, and forgiveness occur daily. Covenant relationships also require the ability to commit to someone for the long haul, which is not easy in today's culture. Fear of commitment in this generation is the result of countless failed marriages and self-centered relationships. But your children also need to know they are not doormats and they are not to make others their doormat. They must understand relational boundaries and what they mean. Therefore, *we* must understand relational boundaries and live according to them with our children, constantly modeling healthy relationships as opposed to lecturing about them, because more is caught than taught in this area. Remember, parenting is first for the maturation of us as parents, then for the children. If our kids learn to love well, they will be able to find happiness and fulfillment in healthy relationships, becoming adept in heart connection and emotional intelligence.

Our children also need to be successful in their life's work. *Work* is a big word that encompasses not only their capacity to provide for themselves but also the ability to chase after dreams and destiny, not allowing entitlement and its best friend, victim mentality, to ensnare them. I believe God created and called each of us to accomplish unique things and this is what gives our lives meaning. Keeping the core mind-set of work and the importance of being industrious will help you as you respond to your child's needs and wants and the way they spend their time and money.

These ultimate goals should drive all our parenting. Loving well and success in life's work are both so important to life, yet they seem to escape much of humanity. I believe that when God created us, He fashioned these goals, including both relationship and accomplishment, two somewhat opposite concepts, to balance out our lives. I also believe that the ability to love well and work successfully are not inherently easy for us humans. We prefer to love selfishly and work as little as possible, or we love insufficiently and work way too much. Either way, this is where our relationship with our Creator God becomes important. The Bible has much to say about these two concepts. If you are approaching your parenting through the lens of God's precepts, you will have the leverage you need as you instill these values in your children in perfect balance. As they see *you* submitted to these principles and understanding, there is a greater authority and power that will call *them* into account as well.

If we as parents allow God to be intimately involved in shaping our lives with love, humility, kindness, and, of course, life's dos and don'ts, we will become more Christlike and avoid those attitudes and choices that are so detrimental to our well-being. As our children allow God a place in their lives to influence everything they do, then we can step back, knowing that regardless of our efforts, the outcome *will* be good. This is because our God causes all things to work together for good for those who love Him.[1]

Always keep in mind that the *ultimate* goals for parenting are to raise adult children who are able to love well and to be successful in work. Regardless of all the pressure to raise champion children, if these two things happen, you're golden.

Never, Ever Break a Sweat

This second parenting fundamental is one I love sharing with parents, especially with those who are at their wits' end. I can't take the credit for this one; it was an amazing bit of life-giving advice that I read in the book *Love and Logic Magic for Early Childhood* by Jim Fay and Charles Fay, PhD. The concept of parenting without breaking a sweat was a game changer for me. It made me step back, take a deep breath, and say, "I'm going to win . . . we are going to be *just fine!*" It may seem crazy to some of you, but choosing to parent without anger, frustration, and yelling is just that—a choice. But to make that choice an actual possibility, or better yet, a reality, we must obtain the tools that are needed to take frustration's place. There are other ways to solve the dilemmas of everyday life with little people in the house! Choose today to set aside the usual exasperation and yelling and, instead, take on a confidence and a strategy that will be much more effective.

When we react to our children's behavior with frustration, angry exasperation, and sarcasm, we are telling them that they are so bad that even we can't handle them. This can become a very strong imprint on their identity. Think about it this way: they are spinning out of control, without the ability to contain themselves, and then their main source of comfort and stability falls apart too! When you are about to lose it, you don't need the person with you to start screaming too! Instead, you need someone there to stay calm and very confident as their nonverbal behavior expresses to you that you are going to be okay and that you aren't able to destroy everything around you; you need them to hold you through it with confidence until you can contain yourself again.

Calm, sweatless parenting also helps the child's relational recovery time. After every behavioral issue, there is the journey back to relationship and right standing with life in general. There is a certain amount of shame and embarrassment one must deal with after acting out. If we as parents enter into their meltdown with anger, saying and doing things that are not fitting, now we will also need to repair the damage we caused to the relationship.

It may sound like a pipe dream to parent a full day without frustration. I know it seemed an impossibility for me too. Either I was to take on extraordinary human powers or I was going to need some extraordinary help. I found that my first step toward sweatless parenting was to pursue the latter! I could not do this on my own, so I began to pray.

Everything that is bothering you about your child most likely bothers your child's heavenly Father as well. You are the agent of change for your child, but God is the one who created them and knows their intricacies. Whether you are a seasoned prayer veteran or more of the SOS type, I encourage you to start by taking your concerns over your child's troubles to the Lord and asking Him to give you the keys to unlock your child's problems. Our kids are more than Pavlov's dog to be trained with rewards and punishments. They are hearts and souls, and if you can gain entrance through empathetic love, wisdom, and prayer, you will find yourself in a very influential place. If you continue to yell and be a crazy, angry parent, I will guarantee your child's heart will be shut down and his soul inaccessible.

God has more than once answered my cry for heart keys and answers, be they practical, psychological, or spiritual. Believe it or not, God has an even greater vested interest in seeing your children overcome than you do! Sometimes the answer to prayer was the revealing of hidden wayward behaviors that affected their attitudes; other times it came in more practical terms. There was a time in Wolfe Cub Number Four's life that found him in a lot of emotional turmoil over school as well as life in general. My husband and I prayed incessantly for an answer, for the key to unlock his heart.

Sterling began to ask us for a dog. I am *not* a dog person, so this seemed out of the question. He then began to ask more specifically for a female chocolate lab named Lilly. Eventually I relented, feeling that maybe this was God's key to his heart. We went to the pound and immediately found a chocolate lab, and the name on her collar was Lilly! We were also surprised to find that after hard homework moments or any other emotionally upsetting situations, Sterling would lie down with Lilly and it would calm him like nothing else. Lilly was God's answer to our prayers and definitely a key to our son's heart.

So, choose to never break a sweat again, standing in quiet assurance that you are bigger than they are and way too mature to join them in their tantrums. Let's enjoy every minute of this parenting thing, relying on great strategies and God's unique insights to navigate those tough moments.

Be the Most Loving, Empathetic Parent in the Universe

Another nonnegotiable mind-set for parenting is the concept of empathetic love. Love is one of the most basic needs of a child, but it's not just any kind of love. Our love must be wise, brave, and courageous.

The first time I laid eyes on my babies, I was *in love*. Love is the incredible glue that holds relationships together. God loves us beyond comprehension. I love my husband beyond words. I love my kids more than you can imagine. Love causes us to hold on through the tough times, stand by when we are fearful, and continue to believe even when we doubt our own capabilities. Love is powerful.

How you express your love to your children is vital to their development. From birth through their first year, they need your love and attention 24/7 for them to develop trust and security. Love during this time is shown through patience, provision, and immediate attention to keep them happy. But there is a transitional moment in every small life sometime between the first and second year when needs become wants.[2] There was a time when your child was originally incapable of holding a bottle, and this is normal. But when your child is old enough to do so yet refuses to hold her bottle, demanding that you hold it, now inability has turned into control. This moment needs to be noted, and your love for your child will take a slight shift. Slowly but surely, you will love them so much that you will begin to limit wants yet continue to meet needs, shifting the responsibility of their happiness upon themselves.

Love is different now. This love sees the value of handling disappointment, waiting, and the concept of *no* in your child's life. This love feels sorry for them as they struggle with these realities. Love now becomes extremely empathetic as to how it feels to lose a toy, a privilege, or time with the family because of poor choices, a lack of self-control, or an act of self-centeredness, yet it doesn't bail them out of their painful predicament. Instead, this love supports them through their pain until they integrate self-control and others centeredness into themselves, because this love knows they will be better off with these things.

Again, *Love and Logic Magic for Early Childhood* encouraged me to know that if I could gently and lovingly respond to my children's choices and protests while holding strong to the expectations, I could set up an environment in which they could learn and mature. Even though your children are angry, they will soften when handled with empathy. If we as parents get angry and frustrated with our children, we set up an environment of fight or flight. You will become their enemy. Their hearts will harden. The battle lines will be drawn.[3]

We all know the struggle we felt as we walked the painful path of maturation. But love knows that the struggle is easier at this point in their lives and will only get harder if postponed. Love at this point says that you, as a parent, are big enough to hold and encompass even their worst behavior without wavering on the expectations, consequences, commitment, or love for them.

To endure the harsh realities of growing up via the real consequences of poor choices, our children need to be rooted and grounded in love (Ephesians 3:17). One day when Wolfe Cub Number Two was a new driver, he took some friends to get some fast food in the family van. All seemed to be well until the next day, when Dad received a phone call from the manager. Apparently, Wolfe Cub Number Two had decided he did not want to simply back out of his parking stall. No, instead he had thought it would be great fun to drive straight ahead, up and over the parking strip in front of him. During this process, he had pulled out some bushes and broke the sprinklers. Fortunately, his mother and father's daily prayer was that their dear children would get caught in every sin they ever committed. Our prayers were answered, because the restaurant had cameras in the parking lot and was able to track down the license plate.

After hanging up the phone, Dwain and I looked at each other. At that moment, we had a lot of feelings and possible action steps that mostly did not include love. This son was in a lot of trouble that we had amply instructed, warned, and begged him to stay away from. After restraining each other from our baser instincts ("I'm going kill him!") we decided to let the situation do the talking, feeling so sad for him as he had to deal with every bit of his actions. He had to purchase sprinkler parts and plants, do the necessary repairs, and apologize to the store owner. Our love for him did not let him get away with anything, yet it didn't camp out in the frustration and anger we initially felt. This was an embarrassing situation for him. We did not yell or get mad at him; we let reality do the talking and we let him know we felt sad that it was hard. Empathy kept us in relationship with Caleb so that he could do the work of learning the painful truth of obedience. It seemed to work—he now dutifully puts his car into reverse and backs out of parking stalls every time!

Your child's anger and frustration in a disciplinary situation should be the only negative emotion. It's our job to handle the situation with loving empathy, the kind that says, "I know this is hard, I feel for you, but you are going to make it through and be so much better for it!"

Establish Healthy Boundaries for Your Children

Another game-changing source of wisdom for me was the book by Henry Cloud and John Townsend, *Boundaries with Kids*. Cloud and Townsend teach that though you can't make your child do anything, you can create a loving environment that encourages some behaviors and discourages others.[4] This means establishing healthy boundaries in your home and family culture. No more power struggles—just rig the system in the favor of great behavior and allow your kids to experience their choices to the fullest.

The subject of boundaries is such an important one in parenting and was so life changing for us in the Wolfe household. I'll spend a little extra time on it and share some of the specific nuggets of wisdom that Cloud and Townsend provided. I also strongly encourage you to read this whole book for yourself!

So, what exactly is a boundary? Here is Cloud and Townsend's definition:

A boundary is a "property line" that defines a person; it defines where one person ends and someone else begins. If we know where a person's boundaries are, we know what we can expect this person to take control of: himself or herself. We can require responsibility in regard to feelings, behaviors, and attitudes.[5]

Notice that a boundary gives people control over themselves, not control over other people. If I come to grips with the realization that I can't *make* my kids do anything, but as a parent, I can set up the environment to favor what I want them to do and highly disfavor what I don't want them to do, then I find myself in a very powerful position. I am no longer trying to control something I have no control over—my children. I can now take control over what I do have complete control over—the environment in which they live.

I have found that many people and *all* children struggle with proper boundaries. When a new human being is birthed, he has no boundaries. There is no *self*-control but there is complete *you*-control. He takes no responsibility, and you have all the responsibility. This is perfectly normal for infants but *not* for adults. The process of giving up control of others and taking control of oneself is a very painful one. It's not easy, but it's one of the most important things that parents can make sure happens in their children's lives. If you have ever met an adult who has poor self-control and yet insists on controlling others, you know what I mean.

So, while the process of establishing boundaries with your children may include pain, Cloud and Townsend explain that this kind of pain is good because it signifies change. We as parents sometimes struggle watching our kids experience pain. It is important to understand that there is a difference between hurt and harm. The pain of hurt is good. We learn we shouldn't do certain things because it hurts too much—costs too much money, costs my independence, costs my privileges. This is very different from the pain of harm. Harm is when irreversible negative actions damage a person (physical abuse and emotional trauma). The tantrum you see as your three- or thirteen-year-old loses her favorite toy or privilege for a time may look like emotional trauma, when actually your child is protesting the pain felt as she processes the need for change. She is not actually being harmed.[6]

Learning self-control, yielding to authority, doing what's right, and limiting our immediate urges are all so painful. There are times even in my fifties when I do not want to do what's right. It's *hard!* But not doing what's right is always more painful! Parenting with boundaries makes sure that if the child does not show self-restraint and does something that is unacceptable, his life will be affected in a negative, painful way. If your child is never faced with the pain of poor choices, he will never learn self-control.

To help you parent with good boundaries, here is a little equation. If you can get it to stick in your head and you run your world by it, it will change everything:

YOU *choose well* = YOU will *live well*

There are incredible rewards for using self-control. Success in every area is just about a guarantee!

The converse is also true:

YOU *choose badly* = YOU will *live badly*

There are incredible consequences for being out of control. Failure in every area is just about a guarantee!

Isn't this how the real world works? *Boundaries with Kids* makes a strong case for the importance of allowing our children to experience the consequences of both good and bad behavior. We all must live with the choices we make. If you choose to get up and go to work, you will receive a paycheck and your life will be better. If you choose to be lazy and don't go to work, you won't get a paycheck and your life will become hard.[7]

Unfortunately, for whatever reason, many parents allow children to choose badly and yet live well. As Cloud and Townsend say, "Too many times, children's behavior does not become a problem for them. . . . Instead, parents allow the problem to become a problem for them instead of their children."[8] This is, in effect, lying to your children about how the universe, in general, operates. You are saying, "Do whatever you want, and I will absorb the consequences so you won't have to."

Notice the rule is NOT:

YOU *choose badly* = I *will live badly* for you so that you can continue to live well

Many parents think this is the kind and loving way to raise children. Yet God, who is the epitome of love, always gives His people choices and does not stop the consequences, good or bad, from manifesting. The above statement is the opposite of boundaries, because it allows the "junk" from their behavior to get on our side of the fence. It's not our job to shovel their messes.

You might be wondering what the second half of that final statement actually means—parents living badly so that children continue to live well. It goes like this: If your child chooses to pitch a fit over being denied a want and you cave and buy it for her, you have taken the financial sacrifice for the item and your child gets to have all the fun. If your child chooses to live irresponsibly and ends up breaking things or harming another's property and you opt to pay for the repairs, the child saves face and you are now living the "bad." It's anytime you take the brunt of the behavior and the child skates off easily. It includes parents paying for car wrecks, broken glasses, and lost phones without any expectation of the child. Accidents are accidents, but if the child is not required to feel at least *some* of the pain, then he or she will not be deterred from future careless accidents.

My question to these parents is this: How far will you go before you stop absorbing the consequences of their bad behavior? My prediction is that you will eventually be supporting them as adults, posting bail, paying for rehab or even a divorce, or perhaps raising a grandchild or two. The sooner you allow children to take responsibility for their actions by allowing them to feel the pain of their choices, the better. Time-outs spent in their bedroom with you as the empathetic warden are much better than time spent at the juvenile detention center at the mercy of an unloving officer!

Healthy parenting boundaries say, "You have a God-given free will to choose anything you want, and I will completely respect that; at the same time, I have a God-given mandate to be sure you are rewarded with the reality of what your choices bring, good or bad, and I will love you the same regardless of your choice."

A great example of this rang true for all four Wolfe cubs when they began to drive. We taught them that it was very important to follow the laws of safe driving so they would not get any speeding tickets or get into any accidents. We told them that as long as they qualified for the good-student discount with our insurance company, we would pay for their insurance, but as soon as their grades slipped or they had enough infractions to warrant being dropped from our insurance policy, they were on their own to purchase high-risk insurance themselves. Three Wolfe cubs fell from grace within their first year of driving. This meant that at the age of seventeen, they were faced with a large insurance bill. It was tough. They were not happy. They had to use their very hard-earned money for insurance instead of the newest gadgets and fancy shoes. At the same time, our bill went down. They chose to drive foolishly and they felt those choices for quite some time. We didn't shield them from this hardship by helping them pay their bills. They chose badly and, therefore, had to live badly. They all survived and have felt the excitement of fulfilling the allotted time, seeing the driving record clear and their bill decrease. It worked wonderfully!

The hope lies in the fact that your cute munchkins will learn that choosing well pays off and choosing poorly is a real pain! Don't bail them out. Instead, love them through their trials of great affliction and they will begin to understand boundaries in a healthy way.

Conclusion

Boundaries, empathy, sweatless parenting, and keeping in mind the ultimate goals of loving well and being successful in their life's work are huge in our monumental task of raising kids. These are the nonnegotiables. There are so many good things that parents want to implement and a never-ending flow of opinions coming at us, but these four foundational keys are more than good ideas or opinions. Every one of our four cubs presented us with unique situations and challenges, but in every situation, these foundational keys rang true and got us through. Be committed to these foundational principles, and you will be heading in the right direction.

Great—we are now set to parent! But I hear you asking, "What do I do when they become obstinate and I start doing the crazy-parent thing?" I will guarantee that your sweet little droplet of perfection will at one point look you in the eye and throw down the gauntlet. At this point, we all need clear direction, things to say, and guidance for action so we don't sink down to our children's level or give them the impression that they are somehow powerful enough to be at our level! Let's look at how you can approach misbehavior in a positive way in the next chapter.

CHAPTER THREE

THE NITTY-GRITTY

Parenting books are always wonderful for inspiration and vision. Taking it to everyday life can become a bit difficult. Book parenting is very neat and tidy, with clear-cut ideas and book children that respond perfectly. But real life is always a bit messier, and real children are unique. Every child and every situation is different, but there seems to be a basic scenario that commonly plays out time and time again. Depending on our parenting approach, this scenario can take two different pathways; one brings success and the other brings frustration. Let's first look at the frustrating path, because it is the most frequently traveled (I know because I have done this one a lot). Then we will look at a more successful pathway and share some wisdom as to how to do things better. Take heart, my fellow parent—your little home can be peaceful, and you and that munchkin can do well in this thing called family!

It all starts with a happy mom or dad and a happy child living life and having a great time, let's say, shopping.

We've all experienced that moment. Your perfectly wonderful child does something that harms the peace and harmonious balance of all things. He decides to have a fit over the toy he desperately wants, but your budget does not allow for such an expenditure. This most likely is not the first time such a moment has arisen. Your child proceeds to throw things and possibly take a swing at you. Your feelings fly from horror to embarrassment to fear of what this will look like in a teenage body. You are frustrated. How could he do this *again*? You are an at-a-loss parent. You then react reflexively with a raised voice, "1 . . . 2 . . . 2½ . . . 2¾ . . ." Your mind searches for some kind of power statement—"If you don't stop crying, we are *going home!*"—knowing all the while you will not leave until you have finished your shopping. You are now sweating, desperate, and powerless. Twenty dollars is not too much to pay for peace, and besides, how important is the budget anyway? Being a tired parent, you pick up the toy and cave to your child's desires.

We have all been there, and if you haven't had this particular experience, I am sure you have had something similar. Amid the mayhem, we must understand an important concept—whenever there is *immediate gratification* (the child gets his way), there is *delayed maturation* (a putting off to a later date his internalization of self-control and character). A few other problems also play into this scenario:

- The child's *adversary and problem* become the angry, sweating parent. The child focuses on *you* because *you* are upset and angry and taking up arms against him.
- The child's *power struggle* is now with the parent instead of with the willful self within.
- The *change* is in the parent's expectation of compliance in the child, not with that willful self within; therefore, the boundary or lesson to be learned remains external as opposed to internal.[9]

There is another way.

Say you are at a friend's house and your sweet little munchkin hauls off and hits your friend's child on the head with a truck. *Love and Logic Magic for Early Childhood* teaches that instead of feeling upset or frustrated, you can actually get excited. You have just been given a fantastic teachable moment! This is just what you have been waiting for![10] You have identified certain acceptable and unacceptable behaviors, and this one is definitely unacceptable. You quickly respond to your child with sadness that now her happy little world is going to have to go bad. You indicate this with a statement of empathy. Fay and Fay recommend something along the lines of "Uh-oh" or "This is so sad." You are a prepared parent, always

TOP TIP #3

Love does not rescue our children from the pain of consequences but walks them through the difficult journey of maturation.

ready to remove items or the child from her environment.[11] You very calmly take away the truck and remove your sweet munchkin from play. When your child screams and cries, you get even happier because you see that it's working. She is realizing that if she makes certain choices, she loses privileges. You are a strong parent and endure her frustration with calm empathy, knowing that you are stronger than any protest she may make. You understand that the hardest thing in the world is to internalize reality, submit to authority, give up control, and take on self-control. You watch as she resolves her angry protest and then becomes sad and, finally, calm. All the while, you are empathetic and sad, yet strong and unchanging.

This scenario is an amazing moment in parenting. Your child is learning that *delayed gratification* (putting off the thing she so desperately wants) produces *instant maturation* (an internalizing of the character traits that are needed to succeed in life) and that self-control causes life to go much better than lack of self-control does.

With this new way of doing things, the following happens:

- The child's *adversary* is now the limit or consequence, and the *problem* is the child's own choice of behavior, not an angry, reactive parent.
- The *power struggle* is within; as the child is denied her desires, it causes frustration and protest inside herself.
- The *change* is within the child as she internalizes the boundary and yields to higher character traits that are so important to success in life (patience, kindness,

truth, obedience) since you are unwavering in the consequence.[12]

So, let's break this down a bit and explore some great thought processes for parents.

1. You are great parents with great kids, living a great life as a great family!

That's a mouthful for sure, and though you might not fully agree with that statement, it is where you must start. First, settle it in your heart that you are great parents—not perfect, but pretty good! Your child is lucky to have you, and God did not make a mistake when He gave you your child. Second, your child is a great kid—not perfect, but pretty amazing all the same! Third, your family life, crazy as it may be, is an incredible place for both parents and children to be. These statements will help you keep a positive perspective as you deal with the challenges of family life.

I remember feeling at times like our children could have done better for parents. Other parents up and down our block were cooler and richer, always going boating or camping. I began to fight back at these untrue feelings by declaring that the Wolfe Pack was the best pack around, always doing fun things and filled with the coolest peeps around (it seemed that the best time for me to joyfully yell these declarations was in our long car rides, headed to a lesson or meeting). My husband and I made it a point to talk about what a great family we were and how blessed we were to have each of us. To this day, I hear these words echoed back from our grown children.

As your children grow into teenagers, they will naturally begin to migrate toward their friends. But if you have molded the culture of your home as a great place to be, they will not venture far before returning back to what is safe, comfortable, and fun.

It's all about your family culture. You have a family culture, whether you know it or not. Your family culture is shaped either by happenstance or by your purpose to make it a place that is wonderful for everyone. To do this, you have to set a standard of honor and respect in attitude and behavior that every family member must uphold, from the three-year-old to the thirteen-year-old to the parent. You get to choose what the culture of your family will be. Many parents merely react to the behaviors of the children, and it seems that the children are setting the tone of the home. Take some time to determine what you want your family culture to look and feel like, understanding that two things will affect it: attitudes and behaviors.

Your family culture starts with attitude. Whether you came from a wonderful family environment or a dysfunctional home, it makes no difference. You can shift your family in the right direction by determining how your family will operate and taking them in that direction. It's a bit humorous: children will believe what you say verbally and nonverbally. Attitude can be heard verbally, but nonverbal communication is where attitudes can really have impact. If you are irritated and frustrated and don't like your family dynamic, they will believe you and take up your drumbeat.

I have a home video that is very sobering. Dwain was

videotaping Jasmine (two and a half at the time) as she sat at the kitchen table singing to herself and coloring, so content and happy, smiling and laughing. I came into the room with an obvious attitude, muttering and a bit negative. She watched and listened to me for about 30 seconds, then her little countenance completely fell. You can literally watch her take on my attitude! She began to act out and get sad. My attitude was reflected in my child. I emotionally impacted her not only with my actual words but also with my nonverbal attitudes. I didn't just affect myself with my bad attitude—I inadvertently set the tone for the culture of our whole family for that moment.

I think it's also safe to say that many times I am perfectly fine and a child with a 'tude can cause me to lose my happy and act out! We all affect each other but we are the adults in the room, and we have the ability to take that deep breath and choose to be happy and calm, processing our challenges and frustrations in positive ways. Whatever was bugging me that day wasn't worth impacting Jasmine's impressionable heart with negativity.

On the other hand, if you are in love with your family unit and talk about how wonderful you each are, your children will develop an internal emotional grid that can support happy attitudes. I think that if we grow up in environments that don't provide this grid, our default heart setting is heaviness and negativity. I know it's not as easy as a few dreamy "Don't worry, be happy" statements. It requires some training for both you and your children. Respect, honor, kindness, and love must be instilled and massaged into each human heart in the home. Invest in the effort to form the emotional culture of your family. It's so worth every bit of work—you will be amazed at what a difference it can make.

Once attitude shifts, behavior should follow. Behavior is a continuum, and you must decide where the line between acceptable and unacceptable lies. Is it okay for your child to hit you? Is it okay for him to whine? Is it okay for him to run in the house? Your child will naturally want to set the acceptability line where he is allowed to do as he pleases— but where do *you* want it to be?

Consider drawing the line at the place that delineates where you or those around you become frustrated. If you aren't feeling respected by your children, then draw the line. We sometimes allow our children to get away with behaviors in the name of "loving patience," or we say it's just a "normal child thing" that they will outgrow. Sometimes we are oblivious, don't know what to do, or are just plain exhausted. Whatever the reason, letting these behaviors go will cause you to develop frustration, then you will eventually blow up. Your blowup will be an overreaction to the behavior at that actual moment. This can breed emotional insecurities in your child as he wonders when the next blowup will come. What's more, your child will be smart enough to know that if he can withstand your blowup and wait for you to go back into "nice" mode, he can then resume his activities as usual. Instead, draw your acceptable behavior lines right at the beginning of disrespect and frustration. Your child will not necessarily outgrow disrespect and disobedience; he will just become more sophisticated in his tactical abilities. Drawing your behavioral boundaries early will teach your children emotional safety in your relationship as well as respect and honor. It will also preserve your nerves—and your natural hair color!

The behavior line goes beyond your immediate family. When your kids start jumping on the couch at your friend's house, you might be fine with it, but does your friend feel frustrated or disrespected? Be diligent to draw those lines in such a manner that you preserve your friend's nerves and your welcome at their house.

Wherever the behavior line is, it must be identified by an easy one-liner. Find something that indicates the crossing over into no-no land. These words must be followed up with an action. If you are consistent and unwavering, your "uh-oh" in public can be enough to change behavior without a scene.[13]

You get to choose. I want to encourage you that what you allow is what you are choosing. Do the homework of making your family culture one of emotional positivity as well as honor and respect. You can do this, and believe me, as time goes on, your children will stand out in the crowd as amazing young men and women, you will reap the benefits of peaceful home life, and society will thank you profusely.

2. Your child will misbehave.

One day I took Jasmine to the mall for her Easter dress. She was two years old and was going have the best Easter finery. Right in the middle of our dress hunt, she found one she wanted, and it was *not* going to work for me. I expected her to totally understand that it just wasn't the right vibe! Instead, my perfect child did the unthinkable: she walked out to the main walkway of the children's section, threw herself on the floor, and screamed at the top of her lungs. It was quite embarrassing, to say the least. Logic, bribery, begging—none of it worked. Somewhere I had read that you should just walk away and ignore your child when she's throwing a temper tantrum, but I didn't want to get arrested for child abandonment.

This just wasn't supposed to happen. She was going to be different from all the other children—she was perfect! I was sweating, shaking, and completely at a loss. I finally scooped her up and took her kicking and screaming to the car.

As perfect as you think those short people who bear your name might be, they really aren't. They will misbehave. If they don't, you may need to take them in for evaluation. At the point of misbehavior, you may tend to feel like a failure; I did. Instead, it's your opportunity to get excited! You get to help your child learn something, and when you are finished with this incident, she will be one tiny step closer to maturity! This is no time for embarrassment, frustration, anger, fear, or feeling hassled or inconvenienced. Instead, put on your calm, happy-for-you-but-sad-for-her, empathetic heart and get to work. Why calm? Because you are bigger than her behavior and you are going to win! Why happy for you? Because on the other side of this, your life will become a tiny bit easier. Why sad for her? Because your child's choice just made her life more difficult, and you really don't want to see her suffer. Why empathy? Because your true empathy shows her that she doesn't suffer alone. Now she doesn't have you to fight against—it's just your child and her choice. Your empathy diffuses her emotions and opens her mind to learning and changing, whereas your anger and frustration will ignite her emotions as she takes up her fight-or-flight response.[14]

3. The pain of consequences is a very good thing.

I love how *Boundaries with Kids* talks about the difference between hurt and harm.[15] As mentioned previously, pain is always the catalyst for change. If your foot begins to hurt, you will change how you walk. If going without your shoes causes your socks to get wet, then maybe next time you will consider putting them on. Hurt is a lasting impression that changes us for the good. Your child going without dinner because he chooses not to eat will hurt but not harm him. He will not die of starvation or malnutrition, but you can bet the next time you say, "Dinner!" he will have a different attitude.

In *Boundaries with Kids*, Townsend warns us of the need to be careful to not superimpose our childhood experiences of harm upon our children's experience of hurt. We must process our own personal harm to raise our children with a better perspective.[16]

Real life is made of consequences. If we don't allow our children to feel the pain of poor choices, we are giving them an inaccurate view of the way the world works. You will not always be there to shield them from real life. If life proceeds as usual, you will most likely die before them, and then who will save them from the pain of reality?

A good consequence is an enforceable one that causes pain for the child and not for you, most often a loss of an item or a change of location.[17] As *Love and Logic Magic for Early Childhood* says, stating consequences is better than engaging in power struggles by telling the child what to do. For instance, don't say, "Pick up your toys"; instead, say, "Feel free to pick up all the toys you want to keep," then proceed to put the toys they don't pick up in an out-of-reach box for a few days. This is a great example of an enforceable statement followed by the consequence of choice.[18]

Unfortunately, I did not read *Love and Logic* until most of my children were grown, but after many yelling sessions with my last born about the clothes all over the floor in his room, I told him that he should, "Feel free to pick up all the clothes you want to keep." He did not believe me and left for school. I did not yell or get into a power struggle with him; instead, I promptly bagged up three garbage bags of clothes after he left. I'm not going to lie, I was smiling slightly as I did it. For the first time, he would be the frustrated one—not me—and I could walk by his room and not feel extremely frustrated and disrespected. That week I empathized with him as best as I could as he washed out his only pair of boxers every day.

Reality-based consequences allow for a calm parent who is free from frustration, a child who is frustrated by the withdrawal of a valued item or event, and a consistent, loving, unchanging parental relationship. This in turn causes changes in the child's behavior to avoid future pain and frustration on his part. Not using reality-based consequences creates a frustrated (and often yelling) parent, a shift away from love and connection, and the return to unwanted behavior after all the dust settles.

4. A wonderful, gigantic protest is a fantastic thing. It means all is going as planned!

It's not easy to tame an out-of-control tiger! Humans are born with *no* self-control. Humans are also born with an insatiable desire to control everyone else and to get their own way. The struggle to yield control of others and take control of self is torturous. If we can see it as progress toward maturation, we are more apt to endure and win as opposed to give in to what our children are wanting.

Our firstborn cub had a will that was made of especially strong steel. At a young age, she would protest for what seemed an eternity. One day at around the age of five, she had a run in with Wolfe Cub Number Two and, consequently, she had to spend some time in her room. What ensued was impressive. She employed every tactic, from yelling and kicking to mean words and throwing things. It seemed I had a tiger by the tail, but I determined to wait out her anger and frustration until she became sad and calm. It felt like it took all day (in reality, it lasted about an hour), but she did finally quiet down. When I came in, she was still a bit angry, but she eventually yielded to my love and we tenderly hugged. I had decorated her room with bunny rabbit wallpaper, and we talked about how soft and tender bunnies were and how life is better when we interact with that same tenderness. She came out of that hard situation a little more understanding of love and maturity. I am so glad I didn't give in and let that tiger out of her room, or we would still be living with tiger tendencies today!

As you endure the struggle, your child is learning that your words mean business. It makes future engagements easier as she realizes that your boundaries are real. It also teaches her that in the real world, there are rules and expectations that are accompanied with rewards and consequences that are really going to happen. I love the following quote from *Boundaries with Kids*:

> **Expect disbelief and testing.** You are implementing a new way for the child to experience the universe, one in which her behavior and her suffering are directly associated with each other. She doesn't have a nagging or raging parent to focus on, ignore, or get around. She has an adult who is now standing back and letting her freely choose for herself how difficult or how pleasant her life will be. This will be an adjustment.
>
> Although your child may argue with you when you present the plan, this is generally not the real test. At that stage she may see your presentation as nagging and tune you out. *It is when you enforce the consequence after she transgresses the boundary that you will see the resistance.* You can expect reactions like shock, disbelief, anger, expressions of hurt and woundedness, isolation, blaming, attempts to pit you against the other parent, and even escalation of the behavior. She is in the middle of a titanic struggle of integrating reality into her soul.

And though she may be making *you* miserable, *she's* not happy, either. The war inside her is far worse than her war with you. Have compassion for that struggle: She is like a sheep without a shepherd, lost in her immaturity (Mark 6:34).

We cannot overemphasize how critical it is at this juncture to stick with the consequences. You may feel guilty, bad, abusive, hated, isolated, overwhelmed, and unloved. Hang on to the boundary! Pray, call friends for support, do whatever you can to stay with it.[19]

Peace and calm will return after the storm. Your child will not be the same. There will be movement toward maturation, however small. How strong-willed your child is will determine how many times you will have to endure, but there will come a time when the protests calm and the self-control begins to grow into good choices. I encourage[20] you to not give up—it will be worth it all.

5. Let's get back to a happy life.

When the protest is over and your child has calmed down, it's time to resume life. *Love and Logic Magic for Early Childhood* advises that you take the child in your arms and hug her. This is a great time to lavish her with piles of more empathy. Say things like "That was so sad!" or "I am so sorry you felt that way!" This is *not* the time for lectures and "I told you so."[21]

I think this was the hardest part for me. I failed many times by giving my children a good lesson on proper behavior, thereby losing the moment of tenderness with them. We need to keep the teachable times separate from the heated moments. Welcome the child back into the family living space and back into the family culture, celebrating the fact that he has just taken another step toward maturity.[22]

CHAPTER FOUR

TRUTH

Sometimes it's easy to parent reactively, responding to the chaos that we want to end—and end *now*! Childish chaos is not fun. The crying, the mess, the inconvenience of incapable little ones—need I list more? But childish chaos is fairly short-lived. Children eventually stop crying, learn how to vacuum, and become skillful with tying their own shoes.

However, foolish living can create another kind of chaos, the kind that lasts until a person's last day on earth. The first three chapters of Proverbs speak about the life of the fool and how much trouble he causes himself and others. The antidote for this foolishness is wisdom, and wisdom is lived out in character, integrity, and values. This is where parenting becomes fun. We get to inscribe into our children's lives the understanding of good things, such as truth, hard work, respect, and manners. Rather than just ridding the bad, we're instilling higher things.

My goal in this book is that my experiences would encourage you to raise your kids not just physically but also spiritually, emotionally, and relationally to higher places. In light of this, we're now going to look at values you can impart to your children. Each topic is filled with fun stories and practical ways in which the Wolfe Den operated. Each chapter will challenge you in your own life as well. Once again, raising children is more about raising us, the parents, first! It's difficult to impart what you do not own. None of us are perfect, and as I continue to read parenting books, I am always challenged in my own life to become more truthful, less entitled, or whatever the current subject may be. As you grow, you will create a culture in your home that is conducive to humility and maturation.

Take these next pages as a launching pad for you to pray into the needs of your child's personality strengths and weaknesses. Ask the Lord to give you answers and ideas to bring both your child and you closer to His heart of wisdom.[23]

The Foundation of Truth

One day when my firstborn was about two years old, she was playing with my magazines on the coffee table. She proceeded to tear them apart, leaving a huge mess on the floor. When I discovered her in the process of attacking the next magazine, I stopped her and asked, "Who made this mess?!"

"Adam!" she replied.

Adam was a family friend that was about her age. The only problem with her story was that Adam lived about fifteen minutes away. When I suggested we find Adam to ask him why he tore up the magazines, she had a hard time finding him. She was stuck. She had to face the truth of who was really behind the destruction. It was hard.

Truth is the linchpin that holds humanity and culture steady. God's very nature is truth, and in Him is no lie. As it says in the book of Numbers, "God is not a man, so he does not lie. He is not human, so he does not change his mind. Has he ever spoken and failed to act? Has he ever promised and not carried it through?"[24] He cannot lie. He cannot stretch the truth. He cannot exaggerate. It is God's Word and the foundation of God's constant state of truth that the universe is set upon. Our relationship with God is based on the truth and fulfillment of His words toward us; if His words were false, then our relationship with Him would be impossible.

It's the same way with us. All relationships are built on truth. Truth builds trust. The level of truth that we operate in with others determines the foundation for the relationship. If our children are to succeed in relationships, they MUST learn to operate in truth, no matter how painful that may be.

When Adam and Eve sinned by eating of the tree of the knowledge of good and evil, their first response was to fear God, hide in shame, then pass the blame with lies.

Then the man and his wife heard the sound of the LORD God as he was walking in the garden in the cool of the day, and they hid from the LORD God among the trees of the garden. But the LORD God called to the man, "Where are you?"

He answered, "I heard you in the garden, and I was afraid because I was naked; so I hid."

And he said, "Who told you that you were naked? Have you eaten from the tree that I commanded you not to eat from?"

The man said, "The woman you put here with me—she gave me some fruit from the tree, and I ate it."

Then the LORD God said to the woman, "What is this you have done?"

The woman said, "The serpent deceived me, and I ate."[25]

When God came looking to be with Adam and Eve, they hid. The relationship was broken. Untruth usually begins with an action that we are ashamed of. Consequently, we want to hide from reality in the form of a lie.

One of my earliest childhood memories was similar. My mom had taken me into the grocery store and I was standing by the bulk candy bins as she shopped. Mom was on a tight budget and I knew she would not want to buy me candy, so I stole a piece of orange-flavored candy. I ran out to the car, climbed in the back seat, and crawled as far under the front seat as possible. I ate it all before she came to the car looking for me. Upon her questioning, I told her I wasn't feeling well (partially true). It took quite a few years before I confessed my wrongdoing. Why is it that hiding and lying come so naturally?

It is critical that we, as parents, are willing to admit our own wrong behaviors and weaknesses instead of playing the victim and blaming everyone else. We need to confess our personal responsibility in our sinful choices. If our children hear us operating in truth instead of blaming others, even when it hurts, they will be more willing to do so as well.

Imagine your child living her adult life struggling with lying. Think of the chaos this foolishness would cause her. As pastors, Dwain and I are privileged to coach people and counsel marriages. We have observed that the many problems people face are based first in misdeeds. However, we've also seen that a spouse often has a harder time forgiving the following deceit than the misdeed itself. Untruth hurts the fabric of a relationship. This realization always inspires me to confront not only misdeeds but also dishonesty at all levels in my own life as well as in my children's lives.

Making Truth Safe

To encourage a culture of truth in our homes, it's important to make truth a safe thing. This can be tricky. We want our kids to be honest about their behaviors and thoughts, but honesty can be scary. Because our basic human nature makes us anticipate rejection from others, honesty requires a certain amount of courage. Sometimes honesty is as simple as being forthright about what you want for lunch. But if there's a family dynamic of criticism or judgment, being able to verbalize an opinion or desire can be difficult. Sarcasm and mockery make being honest and self-revealing of even simple things—like wanting macaroni and cheese instead of peanut butter and jelly—feel unsafe. Consider how each family member treats another's ideas, opinions, and desires. Honor and respect cause us to value each other in these areas and create a safe place to be honest in even the simplest of things.

Quite often, honesty is accompanied with a confession, and this requires even more courage. These confessions can be anything from "I was the one who ate the cookie" to "I stole the money" to "I (fill in the blank with the worst possible thing your child could do)." This is the kind of honesty that we as parents desire. Yet we are in a difficult position: their courage to tell the truth and be vulnerable is preciously important, but we can feel so betrayed by their actions, and justice still requires consequences. How will we react when we hear these confessions? Is the mere act of honesty enough to exonerate the individual from reprisals? If we do impose discipline for the poor action or choice, will that reinforce the need for dishonesty the next time?

First, we need to come to a place in our hearts where our children can't hurt us or surprise us with even the worst

TOP TIP #4

Truth provides the groundwork for healthy relationships. The more truthful a person is, the greater his or her relational abilities will be.

kind of truth. When you solidly live in this state of mind and heart, your response to your children's truth will not be reactionary. Now you are creating a safe environment for those in your family to express themselves honestly. If we as parents react and the child experiences a perceived loss of love, he will play it safe and lie. Instead, if we lovingly and compassionately listen, rewarding truth with empathy and thankfulness, he will feel safe and find courage to be truthful. At the same time, we also must enforce consequences that are equal to the behavior and attitude shown. Our love for our children is bigger and stronger and more capable of holding them through even the worst of their actions when we don't react to their truth but instead lovingly hold them through what can be difficult times.

This brings us back to the concept of sweatless parenting. We start by not breaking a sweat with our toddlers when they lie about their magazine-ripping skills, accuse someone with a solid alibi, and expect you to believe it. The concept of boundaries and reality-based consequences must still be enforced with the utmost empathetic love. We continue with sweat-free empathetic love through the very tough years as our teens do things that would shock the best of us. Take courage that you can hear truth and still love your child while allowing reality-based consequences to have their intended effect.

Feelings and Truth

It's important to help your children understand that it's okay to feel a certain way, but sometimes those feelings are not based on truth. Your child may be completely terrorized by the notion that there are monsters in her closet. Her fear is real, but it is not based on truth. Continuing to reinforce the emotional safety of your home by validating her feelings while gently helping her understand the truth of a certain situation allows your child to experience new feelings that are based on that truth. When your child realizes there are no monsters in the closet, then the feelings of confidence and comfort can return. This seems like a no-brainer when we are speaking of monsters in closets, but the concept of keeping our feelings based on truth will be important to carry into adulthood.

Speaking of feelings, Dr. John Gottman writes in *Raising an Emotionally Intelligent Child* that we also must help our children understand that though all feelings are acceptable, not all behaviors are acceptable.[26] It's okay for your child to feel sad that he must share the toy he wanted, but it's not okay to hit his brother. As you help your child see the truth that sharing doesn't mean a forever loss of the toy, he can now base his feelings on this truth as well as exercise stronger self-control.

Finally, it's also important to show our children that our relational connection with them is bigger than their behavior failure. Your child must know that it's okay to be upset about a situation that she finds herself in and that being truthful about her failure will not injure your relationship, even though it may make you sad.

Raising kids for over twenty-five years has given Dwain and me plenty of opportunities to watch our kids in times of misbehavior and untruth. We've constantly prayed that the truth would always come out. It's been almost humorous how the Lord has been faithful to that request. It seems our children have not been able to get away with much!

We also asked God for incredible amounts of intuition and perception. When I am uneasy, there is always a reason. One time when one of the Wolfe cubs was in their teen years, I knew they were hanging with the wrong crowd, and I was concerned. I walked by them one day and mentioned I smelled something. I wasn't smelling what they thought I was smelling, but that statement alone made this particular Wolfe cub confess their wrongdoing. It was wonderful! I didn't have to interrogate or accuse, and our relationship wasn't strained by an ensuing battle for honesty.[27]

One way to keep your home a safe place for truth is to avoid accusing your child. If you call your child a liar, you will only incite defensiveness and encourage conflict. However, if you simply say, "I have a hard time believing you," you are giving your child the opportunity to confess and separating his behavior from his character—he may be lying, but you still believe he can be an honest person.[28]

As we make our relationships safe for truth, things will come out. It is important that instead of reacting, you praise your child for his honesty, then express great empathy for the consequences. It might mean visiting those your child harmed, like the friend's dad regarding repayment for the taillight his fireworks blew out. It might mean repairing the parking lot bushes he ran over with the family van while being filmed by the restaurant owners. It might mean returning stolen goods. As you support your children through the situation and allow the consequences to remain separate from your relationship, you will teach your children some incredible lessons in honesty.

One more thing: we all know what a lie is, but there is a vast amount of gray area between a full truth and a full lie. You can call it exaggeration or just not full truth, but whatever you call it, your children must learn that even gray-area dishonesty is wrong, and they must grow up celebrating full truth. Make it a family value to be truthful in all things, even on the size of the fish that got away!

As you make honesty a valued characteristic of your family, you will see incredible, far-reaching effects in your children's lives as they enter adulthood. It wasn't easy to bring our kids to a place of embracing honesty. I remember a moment in one cub's life that indicated a shift toward truthfulness. This particular cub was in seventh grade and taking advanced math classes. We were on a family vacation over Christmas break when my son came to us and confessed he had been completely cheating his way through algebra. He was realizing how deep his deception was becoming and how hard it was going to be to get back on track; he appeared to be an A student, but in reality, he was falling further and further behind in the concepts. I was so thankful for his courage to be transparent; we then took steps to correct the situation. It was hard for him to bear the burden of untruth, yet it was so good for him to learn how to lay it down in honest conversation. My son's math proficiency was important, but as time went on, it became even more important as he eventually began schooling for engineering. Cheating and lying in his academic life could have altered his future!

Take the time to be vigilant in this area of truthfulness and transparency. You will be so glad that you did the work while your children were young.

CHAPTER FIVE

HOW WE APPROACH OUR LIFE'S WORK

All of us can benefit by asking ourselves, Who is responsible for my life? You might think that's a crazy thing to ask, but for many adults, this is a pivotal question. Am I solely responsible for all things "me"? If anything good is going to happen, am I going to have to do it myself? Am I just a product of what others have or have not come through on for me? Either one of these approaches can cause great anguish and can bring a lot of chaos into life and parenting. The true answer lies somewhere in between. Let's take a look at the possibilities and hopefully shed some light on things.

Being successful in life's work is incredibly important to the formation of a healthy adult child. As you may remember, it is one of the ultimate goals of our parenting! Complicating this goal is the fact that every child has a different disposition when it comes to her approach to work. Some love the challenge and rise to the occasion with illustrious effort. Others moan and groan as if we are killing them. Depending on your children's natural dispositions and how you approach them, the resulting adults can be drastically different. On the one hand, you may have a laissez-faire, passive person, dependent on other people. On the other hand, you may have a works-driven, earned-love kind of person who is stubbornly independent, not needing or wanting help from anyone to succeed. Neither are good; we are aiming for somewhere in between. You are aiming for an adult child who is interdependent, allowing others to contribute their advice and help as she initiates and takes responsibility for success.

Let's break down the difference between a passive child and a stubbornly independent child.

Passivity

Passivity can be part of a child's personality as well as a learned behavior. As a personality, it has its positives and negatives. A calm, easygoing child is very easy to parent. He goes with the flow and doesn't make too much of a ruckus.

I have a somewhat-easygoing child. Our Austin was such a fun, lighthearted kid, always bridging the sibling relationships with laid-back interactions and a happy smile. Every day for school lunches I packed each child three carrots in a little baggie. Through a series of events, it became apparent that Austin was the only one who actually ate them—the rest of the lovely children threw them away each day! Easygoing compliance can be nice at times.

But don't confuse personality with learned behavior. Passivity as a behavior is not so wonderful. Passivity as a learned behavior is characterized by procrastination, ignoring instruction, lack of initiative and risk, inward fantasy-world orientation, and isolation.[29] These behaviors do not bode well with future employers or spouses!

When Austin was very young, we began to notice that his laid-back personality often led to passive behavior. His first question in the morning was, "Caleb, what are we going to do today?" His older brother Caleb would proceed to line out everything they would play, even down to what Austin would need to say and do in their playacting. Though it was cute and Caleb enjoyed being in charge, it set up Austin for difficulty when Caleb started school. I watched as Austin had to engage and make choices and plans, finding himself as he was required to make his own way. It was painful at times, as he had to try hard to come up with fun ideas for himself, but taking on the responsibility of his own world was a very good thing.

Passive behaviors have many causes and various parental responses. If you have a child who is stuck in passivity, I encourage you to read all you can on the subject! In the meantime, here is my take on what to do, based on what I learned in *Boundaries with Kids* and from our own life experiences:

1. Be a parent who is active. The best way a child can learn is by your own example. As she sees you

dream, problem solve, and accomplish ideas and assignments, she will be inspired!

2. Don't rescue him. "Love and grace are free, but everything else in this world must be earned!" Let him feel the pain of the consequences of procrastination and missed deadlines.

3. Require problem-solving. She wants you to do all the work, and I suppose you are free to do it all for her, but if you find yourself working harder than she is, then you are not doing her any favors. In fact, you are reinforcing her lack of initiative and producing inactivity. Why should she worry when the parentals will take care of it? Instead, ask her, "What's your strategy?" or "What are you going to do about that?" Sometimes she cannot connect the dots as far as planning; if that is the case, give her a few ideas, but insist that she decide and take the needed steps to accomplish her desires.

4. Make passivity painful. Let him know that if he tries and fails, you will be there to help, but if he does not try, then he is on his own.

5. Allow time for the process. Passive children will need more time and more patience than the rest. Be sure that you reward even small steps and efforts toward problem-solving.[30]

Your main concern needs to be getting these kids thinking, moving, and interacting. Don't allow them to isolate so much that they become unskilled interpersonally. While they may never be the outgoing life of the party, they can be interactive and self-supporting, fulfilling the wonderful purpose God has for them.

Stubborn Independence

The other extreme on the personality continuum is being stubbornly independent. Like passivity, independence is a personality type as well as a learned behavior. Independence means to not depend on someone else for what you need; in other words, you are self-sufficient. The children who function in independence naturally can also be a blessing to parents. They learn skills easily and quickly and are very glad to do them. They seem to know what needs to be done and are quick to jump in and get it done. They are always dreaming and scheming of their next adventure, and nine times out of ten, they make it happen.

When these children begin to refuse any advice, training, or help, they transition into stubborn independence. The problem with the stubbornly independent person is that she is her biggest limitation. Whatever she doesn't know, she isn't going to ask about or research. Instead, she will plow ahead and make a ton of mistakes.

Boundaries with Kids speaks of two types of good dependency that are true of all of us: functional dependency, in which we need others' help in performing tasks, and relational dependency, which is our need for connectedness with God and others. In their quest for functional independence, stubbornly independent children can find it difficult to remain relationally dependent. A big concern for these children will be their ability to rely on God. We all have limitations and failings that hinder us. Humanity is united in the realization of our finite place in a very large, daunting world. We also know the feeling of needing outside help and support from something bigger than ourselves to do the things life demands of us. The ability to come to the end of ourselves and rely on God is a big step in humility and trust. The stubbornly independent will not be willing to do this naturally.[31]

Here are a few suggestions for parenting a stubbornly independent child, some taken from *Boundaries with Kids* and some being my own:

1. Work to stay emotionally connected to the stubbornly independent child. He will experience a lot of frustration as he comes to terms with the fact that he is not omnipotent, nor does he have control over all things. Huge doses of empathy and a refusal to abandon him will have an amazing effect.[32]

2. Be a learner and a seeker of knowledge yourself. Once again, it's easier to be an example than a lecturer.

3. Model and teach how to be dependent on God and rely on Him, not only when you can't do something but also when you can. Give Him all the glory and continually count your blessings.

4. Have a lot of love and patience. Allow for mistakes, because there will be a ton!

5. Ask questions like, "What's your strategy?" and "What will happen if . . . ?" This will help your child think about his plans and possibly identify the help he needs.

6. Be there for the crash and burn. Try not to lecture, but wrap your child with loving arms and coach her heart.[33]

Cub Number Four would fall in the stubbornly independent child category. He was always doing huge things at a very young age. At age six, he was in the backyard rallying all the neighbor kids to form a work party to build a tree fort. When he was 17, he crashed his '75 Toyota truck he had bought thirty minutes prior—then he got it in his head to rebuild it. We were very proud of him for his grit and determination throughout that summer as he toiled in the backyard, putting in a new motor, finding replacement parts, doing the bodywork, and getting the thing back on the road. His biggest problem, though, was that he detested asking for help. His father gave advice here and there, and quite often it went unheeded. I am happy to say that after many months, it was a drivable vehicle. However, there were lots of snags, redos, and extra bolts and thingamajigs lying around after he was finished. There were the added costs of fixing all the problems that his oversights caused. It was hard for him to learn that he had limitations and that he needed help and advice to really be successful, but the lessons learned were priceless in bringing his stubborn independence into the new realm of interdependence.

Interdependence

Interdependence is the solution to the negative aspects of both passivity and stubborn independence. When our children function in interdependence, they are able to consider what they can and cannot do, doing what they can and getting help with what they can't. This requires them to be strong enough to try things and humble enough to admit they need help.

Being interdependent, actively pursuing great things with others' help, can become a key aspect of your family culture. Here are a few action steps we took in the Wolfe Pack to achieve this value:

1. Dream big and walk the talk. Teach your kids to think outside the box and then research ways to make it happen. Model how to be a can-do person, not a can't-do person.

2. When you as the parent find yourself stuck in inability, admit it! Talk about your reliance on God and your need to learn from other people. We made sure our kids knew we had limitations as well as a great love of gaining insight and help from others.

3. Every time you hear your child voice a need, get him to voice a strategy. Getting your child to take his dreams and connect them with action steps will help him turn vision into reality.

4. Turn off the TV! TVs and tech screens, in general, are brain Binkies. They pacify us into thinking we are something great when we haven't thought a single original thought! We do not have the TV on as background noise in the Wolfe Den. If there is something on, then we will watch it—occasionally. This will keep everyone engaged and talking and, better yet, thinking! There are times when our screens can help us in our journey of accomplishment. YouTube videos helped Sterling countless times as he rebuilt that truck. Positive and helpful programming can be beneficial—just make sure you are all staying away from the constant use of screens in your daily

lives.

Interdependence is powerful for humanity. In passivity, our limitation is what others aren't doing for us. In stubborn independence, our limitation is what we cannot do on our own. In interdependence, relying on our initiative and the wisdom and help of others and God, there is no limitation to what we can do. Take time to evaluate your children and be brave enough to tackle their propensities to migrate toward the outside edges of the continuum. Consider the ways I suggested to pull them in toward the balanced middle, and watch for yourself as your children mature into greatness.

TOP TIP #5

When we live in interdependence, we are courageous enough to use our own resources yet also humble enough to seek out others' assistance.

CHAPTER SIX

CHORES: KEEPING IT A TEAM EFFORT

One day a few years back, I was out working in the yard. It was a beautiful day and the neighbors were all out as well. One was mowing the lawn, and when they stopped to empty the bag, they called out to me about how hard they were working. I called back, "Yep, that's why I have kids!" About an hour later, one of my sons came out and mowed the lawn. The next weekend, I saw the same neighbor out with their teenager, giving a lawn-mowing lesson.

Kids can fly under the work radar if we let them. But they are young and strong. Why should we do all the work while they play?!

I understand the developmental importance of play in our children's lives, but I believe there is also developmental importance in learning how to work and contribute to the common good of community. It seems that the former often gets all the attention and the latter gets overlooked. It's also important for our children to contribute to the family with a happy heart. This requires them to take on compassion and care for the family and each individual member.

Don't get the wrong impression. My teenagers did not come forth from the womb with their work gloves on, just waiting for their opportunity to become contributing members of our familial society. We had many moments of whining, complaining, fussing, wrangling, and plea bargaining before we experienced joyful participation.

I am absolutely convinced that after my casual comment, my neighbor across the street and their teenage son had a long and protracted debate. I can't tell you for sure, but it quite possibly included some pushback, frustration, bribery, and perhaps even dirty looks. Maybe that only happened at my house—the neighbor's kids always did seem like the perfect type—but most likely your kids are more like mine. If so, take courage. As the household and yard naturally deteriorate each week and your parental lives only become more demanding, you can recruit those strapping young piles of potential to your family team. You can get the help you need, and they can learn some valuable character traits!

My father was one of five kids growing up in Leavenworth, Washington, on the family orchard and farm. In the early 1930s, tough times hit. His dad took a job in Seattle and his mom had to work out of town as well. At the ripe old age of seven, nine, eleven, thirteen, and fifteen, those kids ran the farm, pruned the trees, harvested the apples, and cared for the livestock as well as kept up with school and cooked for themselves. None of them died, none of them needed adult psychiatric treatment, and all of them were very successful in their life's work. Those kids grew up to be amazing, can-do, hardworking, responsible adults, part of what was later known as the Greatest Generation. Kids are far more capable than we give them credit for.

My father's life may have been a bit extreme, but all the same, I want to encourage you to instill in your children a work ethic. But let's not stop there—let's encourage them to love work. Work is not a four-letter word. I started early, making it a point to tie chores with teamwork, fun, family, and reward (namely, money). Before you judge me, let me outline how I did this. Feel free to pick and choose, laughing at what won't work for you and thinking of the ways it will work. Whatever you do, do something! It will greatly benefit you and your child.

Let's start with chores.

Chores can be a struggle for a family. Yet I see it as the lifeblood of family culture, work ethic, and the survival of the parents' sanity. It all depends on how you approach it, when you start, and what strategy you employ. Here are a few things we did at the Wolfe Den.

Kitchen Duty

Some families assign a rotating kitchen duty to one person a week. Other families are content to allow the mom or dad to do all the dishes all the time. Kitchen duty can be a real problem or a real win, depending on how you approach it.

Doing the day's dishes was quite possibly the best part of the Wolfe day (at least in my book).

Stop! Don't throw your book down in disbelief quite yet. Hear me out. Believe me, after-dinner cleanup started out as one of the worst times of my day. I was tired, and the kids were all wound up, wanting to run off and play and leaving me with a new mess in the sink. I needed help, and they were the most practical people to come to my rescue, since they had just eaten all the wonderful food that made all the mess! It took us a long and patience-testing journey of setting forth expectations and training attitudes, but it paid off.

TOP TIP #6

Creating a family team dynamic for household chores develops comradery and a sense of community as everyone pulls together.

The key to our efforts was making the kitchen cleanup enjoyable. We incentivized the work by holding a family baseball game, sock-ball war, or wrestling match after dinner. Eventually, kitchen cleanup turned into a time when we all stayed in the kitchen and laughed and sang and did the dishes together. Some of my favorite memories are of dinner-dish doing, and the tradition still stands today! We had lots of fun joking and hip bumping as someone blasted the music and danced. It stretched out family dinner interaction another fifteen minutes or so, and no one person was stuck slaving away. Always remember: if you are happy, your children will eventually follow suit!

We had one rule: nobody leaves till the dishes are done! This rule was not always quoted with grace and love. Each cub tried their hardest in their own unique way to avoid participation at one time or another, while the rest of us called them out with our best God voice, *"Nobody leaves!"* No matter who was pulling a fast one, I just kept bringing things back around, trying to not allow anyone special treatment and all the while keeping the goal in mind.

Here are some helpful hints as you launch into your own version of happy kitchen family times.

1. Make the kitchen kid friendly. Get a stool so short people can reach the sink. Box up the fancy dinnerware from the wedding and go buy some cheap, indestructible Corelle dishes, allowing for bumps and bangs without the pain of loss.
2. Start off when your children are old enough to carry their plates to the sink. Take advantage of those early years of them wanting to "be a helper." It's okay if they spill or drop something—just help them clean it up and cheer them on the next time.
3. Teach your children to say, "Thank you for the good dinner. May I be excused?" when they are finished eating. This keeps those young 'uns from running off to their own thing and teaches them to honor everyone with their attention. If you are done with family dinnertime, then excuse them from the table to start the dishes.

4. The age of the child determines the kitchen duty. In our family, this started with the youngest carrying their plate to the sink. As they grew older, we added on clearing the table and putting things away. Then they rinsed the dishes with a partner helping to load them into the dishwasher. Finally, when they were able, they could wash, dry, and put away the pots and pans. Somewhere in there was the fine art of boxing up the leftovers and getting those counters wiped down. Everyone had a job, so the work was done quickly.

5. Get some fun music playing, sing loudly, throw a towel or two, and remember: *nobody leaves!*

Housecleaning

I chose to do my housecleaning on Saturday mornings. Each child was assigned not only personal responsibilities (namely, their room and personal belongings) but also general household chores that benefited the whole family, which were doled out as they became older. Each year or two, the chores would bump down to the next kid and the oldest would take on something new. This worked great until the first three were gone. Poor Sterling! He ended up with a pile of chores when his brothers moved out. Don't worry—once he realized his list was stacking up, he protested and I shifted some things back onto my list.

Dwain and I are early risers, and we don't value sleeping in past 6:00 or 7:00 a.m., no matter what day it is. We got the kids up by 8:00 a.m. at the latest, encouraging joy with fun music and Saturday-morning waffles or crepes. I had their lists ready with age-appropriate jobs. We would all work together, keeping the music going. Our cubs got very efficient and quick about it because we quite often had something fun planned for lunchtime, such as a hike or a visit to the park.

The following is a loose list of my cubs' housecleaning chores. Feel free to adapt it to your family's needs.

Younger Children
- Stock toilet paper in each bathroom
- Empty garbage in bedrooms and bathrooms[34]
- Fold towels

Older Children
- Dust
- Vacuum the cars
- Mow, edge, and blow the yard as a team
- Sweep the walkway
- Pick up other assigned living spaces
- Vacuum
- Clean the kids' bathroom

The trick is to start 'em young! By the time they know better, it will be just what the family does. If you are past the "start 'em young" timeframe, then start 'em now—it's never too late! It will take some strong, patient determination on your part as well as some divine wisdom as to specific motivators that will speak to their hearts. No matter what season you are in with your family, make at least one course adjustment regarding chores. The results will be wonderful.

Laundry

Laundry seems to be a living monster that wants to invade *every* square inch of the home. I personally preferred to get it done in a day and not have constant piles screaming to be folded. Call me crazy, but I would do seven to eight loads of laundry on laundry day. I am *not* saying that is the only way to go. I found out later that some of my friends passed off the children's personal laundry to each of them individually around the age of ten to do for themselves. I don't think that would have worked for us, but you could give it a try.

Each child had a different-colored basket. On the morning of laundry day, the cubs were responsible for bringing me their basket of dirty clothes. If I found they were just scooping up clean clothes from their floors that they just didn't feel like folding, I set them aside and challenged them to "Show me the dirt!" or pay me to wash their clean clothes. After a few times of giving me their hard-earned quarters, that behavior was extinguished!

When the kids were early-elementary age, I really got inspired with this chore thing. I figured folding clothes was a great place for the kids to jump in. I saved piles of clean clothes for them to do after school, mostly socks, underwear, and towels—the easier stuff. Tuesday was laundry day as well as the day we hosted a small group at our house in the evening. One day they completed their laundry tasks in record time. That evening, as our guests found their seats in our living room, they felt certain strange lumps under their cushions. One by one, our guests began to pull out underwear, boxers, socks, and other various personal items that had been stuffed under the pillows and cushions by some intelligently sneaky children. It was then that I began to realize that maybe I was asking a little much of them. I dialed it back to more realistic expectations on the folding thing.

As time passed, I would wash and fold most of the laundry, at least getting it into their personal baskets; I did not like waiting for them to fold their clothes themselves. You really have to choose your battles, and this was one that didn't cause me too much frustration. The cubs were responsible for taking their baskets up to their rooms and putting away the clothes. If laundry is your least favorite thing, then maybe you could devise a solution to better meet your needs, but this worked for us.

The day the cubs graduated from high school was the last day I did a load of laundry for them. In reality, a few of them started doing their own laundry before that fateful day, but you get the picture.

Involve your children in the laundry tasks in a way that fits your lifestyle. Your life will be easier, and they will begin to understand the work involved in that clean shirt they just pulled out of the drawer!

Make It Your Own

I am sure there are plenty of other ways to do chores. Be creative. Be sure you have fun while you do them. Life is crazy. If you work full-time, you're likely tired when you get home, so I recommend you have a good chore plan so you can get some relief. But tired or not, set aside your stress and have fun. If *you* are loving chore life, your kids will too. If you hate work, chores, and life in general, your kids will as well.

Every normal child will complain and fuss. Overcome your children's protests with empathy, laughter, humor, and lots of fun. Attitudes are contagious; it really comes down to whose attitude will win. Will it be their stinky one or your happy one? Be the stubborn one on this. Don't give in and join them. Make them join you!

CHAPTER SEVEN

KIDS AND MONEY

Money and kids—it's an interesting relationship. They think it grows on trees that are constantly in season. It is a very painful process to come to the realization that money isn't there for the pickin' but instead must be made.

One day, my three-year-old firstborn was asking where her daddy was. I replied, "At work." Her next question was what he did at work, and my reply was, "Daddy goes and makes money for us." A while later she wanted me to show her this money machine her dad had so that she could make some herself.

Cub Number One's misunderstanding was cute at the moment because her young mind pictured more of a counterfeiting operation than a legally profitable business. But actually, she was onto something. She was not asking to be given money but was inquiring about how to generate money. If she learned how to generate money instead of getting it showered upon her, she would also learn the value of money.

Getting our kids to generate their own money and learn the value of every buck through proper management is a very tough process. Every one of my cubs much preferred to be given all things they desired immediately—if not sooner! This created a lot of frustrating moments for Dwain and me. We wanted to be the cool parents our kids would love, yet the budget did not allow us to keep up with everyone around us. Saying no to things earned us some choice words and bad attitudes at times. Either we were going to take the pain of the unwanted financial pressure by saying yes to their wants or we were going to have good boundaries, say no, and put the responsibility of their own wants upon their shoulders.

But simply saying no to things they wanted could not be the end of the story. That would have taught our kids the hopeless feeling of poverty and can't-do spirit when it came to their dreams and desires.

If you provide everything your children need *and* want, then there is no inspiration to dream for something, work hard, and save for it. They will never feel the satisfaction of finally purchasing that highly valued item, bringing it home, and—most importantly—taking very good care of that item. I want to encourage you to say no to things and allow them to feel the pain of waiting and earning something. The gifts and blessings we bestow on our children are sometimes more for our benefit. We want their love too much, or we might be fulfilling our own childhood dreams through them. It is important to allow our children to feel the tension of unmet wants in a positive environment. This will drive them to seek industrious ways to fill those unmet wants and desires. If your children do not have any unmet needs, then money means nothing to them. The rest of this chapter rests in this pretext.

But before we get into the practical how-tos, I want to take a moment to address the families who are financially strapped. I get it. I was raised by a single mom on a fixed income that was below the poverty line. It's tough. But don't be discouraged. This is where the information I am about to share can become exciting. It's not about spending money to give our kids things; it's about inspiring you to help them discover ways to create and manage money well. Because of how my mom taught me to approach life, I came out of childhood believing that if I wanted something, I could figure out how to go about making the money to get it. Read the rest of this chapter with the mind-set of figuring out how it can work for you. Your situation may be different from mine, but the principles remain the same. Valuing money and entrepreneurialism are very important to your child's success in life.

Learning the Value of Money

Learning the value of money can be done only if it is tied to your children's own blood, sweat, and tears. Personally, I didn't want to give my children money every week just because they existed. They were all able-bodied and strong, just young and inexperienced. I also got very tired of buying them gum and treats at the store. I fed them all the food they *needed*; it was time they took responsibility for their *wants*. For this to work, a flow of income had to be established. In addition, every bit of leverage in their behavior was always welcomed. By the time my oldest was around five years old, I also needed another vehicle for rewards and consequences—hence my trip to the bank for some rolls of coins.

Those rolls of nickels, dimes, and quarters were my new incentive for money management and good behavior at the Wolfe Den. Keep in mind that at this point, family chores were just what we did. The previously mentioned system of housework and laundry continued without being tied to money. I didn't want them thinking that they would be getting paid for everything. Believe me, each child tried to negotiate pay for any and all chores at one time or another. My quick response was that if I had to pay them to clean their room, then dinner that night would cost them five dollars. It worked like a charm. I also threw in the fact that we did our regular chores around the house because we were a team and we loved our family.

When I wanted a child to take on a new chore that would be challenging to them or I possibly just wanted something out-of-the-ordinary done, I would "hire" them. They could accept the job or not, but keep in mind that I always knew the things my kids were wanting and saving for, and that was always my way of motivating their cooperation. This is why our children always need to have an unmet want, a dream item that you won't just give them. If they accepted my job, I taught them how to do that job and told them to come get me for an inspection when they were finished. I allowed them one free inspection, but if a second inspection still did not show good effort, I began to charge them for my time. This concept of charging for my time to oversee their workmanship worked perfectly if I started getting poor effort on their Saturday-morning chores as well. After the job was done, I would pay them in dimes and nickels and quarters. They would then pay me for any additional inspections, if applicable.

The cubs had jars or envelopes to keep their money in, one jar each for savings, tithes and offerings, Christmas gifts, and fun. As they got older, sometimes those extra paid jobs became unpaid, regular jobs, but I tried to always have something they could do extra for cash. This way, they could use their fun funds for the gum and chips they were always wanting at the store, letting me stay out of the business of loaning my cubs money at the checkout.

This worked wonderfully, but it wasn't long before their "wants" became more expensive and it was apparent that a financial stream outside of our home would be beneficial. New money was an amazing concept.

Entrepreneurialism

Now let's focus on leading our children into the concept of generating money for themselves.

The book of Ecclesiastes says, "money is the answer for all things."[35] I suppose that could be debated, but I can see the point. It doesn't take long for those cute little babies to start wanting bigger and better toys. Eventually, they will

want $200 tennis shoes, $300 purses, and $700 phones.
The countdown to the big sixteenth birthday and ensuing
driver's license will lead to needing a car. And it doesn't
end with a car. There's insurance, gas, traffic tickets, and
insurance deductibles for every crash. Either we as parents
will foot the bill or we will help our children find a pathway
to earn it themselves. We can buy them the stuff they want
or buy them the means to earn the money to buy the stuff
they want. Dwain and I chose to invest in our cubs, setting
them up to make money.

Start your children young with their ability to earn
money by working around the house, as stated earlier. Don't
buy them everything they want. Say no. Require them to
earn some things. They must learn how to live without
having every want fulfilled, yet knowing that every need
will be met. Let them spend those hard-earned quarters on
that bag of chips they must have and then realize that when
the money runs out, so does that luxury.

Love and encourage any entrepreneurialism they
show. Who knows if that lemonade stand might be the
beginning of something big? Instead of hating the mess and
inconvenience, do what you can as a parent to encourage it
and then celebrate the money it earns.

Think outside the box as your children begin to grow
up. Get them certified as babysitters, complete with a CPR
class. Help them create a name for their business, and show
them how to market themselves with flyers and business
cards.[36] Take their natural gifting and talents and turn them
into businesses.

My daughter took years of piano lessons; in ninth grade, she shifted over to the harp. After a year of harp lessons and a harp rental (my investment into her profit-earning pathway), we printed up full-color flyers with a picture of her and her harp, and out she went to businesses around town, offering her services. Her first gig paid $125 for an hour. Not bad for a sophomore in high school! She went on to play side jobs, putting herself through college.

TOP TIP #7

Instilling a mindset of wealth generation in our children bestows them with a lifelong gift that will set them apart in adulthood.

When my first son turned twelve, we helped him start his business. He was very adept at mowing and edging our lawn by that point (chores are a wonderful thing). We made some refrigerator magnets[37] for Caleb's Affordable Lawn Service. He posted flyers throughout the close neighborhoods and came up with three weekly jobs at $15 apiece. That was $180 per month. Pretty good for a sixth grader in 2002!

That spring, a group of young men came through our neighborhood, thatching and aerating lawns for a very affordable rate. We hired them and watched as two high schoolers made $75 from us in about thirty minutes before they ran to the next neighbor. My husband and I looked at each other and said, "Genius!" When Caleb was fifteen and Austin was twelve, we made up flyers for Wolfe

Bros' Thatch-n-Patch. They posted the flyers around the surrounding neighborhoods. They hated every minute of it, and they even threw flyers in bushes to appear like they had finished their task! But soon we got our first calls. My husband scheduled a Saturday with a few jobs and rented a thatcher and aerator, and off they went. Dwain had to teach them the ropes, drive them around, and deal with the customers, but they came home with money in their pockets, blisters on their hands, and a lot of excitement. Eventually they bought their own equipment, and they soon took over the scheduling. My husband spent many hours driving, repairing, training, and coaching, but my boys now have a strong work ethic, a mind for business, personally paid-for cars, and very *little* college debt.[38] That business is still going today. At the writing of this book, Austin is thatching and aerating on his days off in Boise, Idaho; Caleb is working his side business in Longview, Washington; and Sterling is still servicing our local long-term customers here at home.

I know this all may seem a bit crazy. It will take up some of your time as a parent to help them get started, but creating a pathway for your children to create work and wealth will be a total game changer for you and for them! You don't have to do a harp or lawn business like we did. Ask the Lord for guidance and be creative. Your kids are very capable of great things. Don't dummy them down. Push them forward.

Conclusion

Whew! That felt like a lot of information! Getting our

kids on the right page as far as money goes is nothing short of miraculous. In reality, it's hard for even us as adults! Yet valuing the importance of a hard-earned buck just might be one of the greatest gifts we can give our children. Money doesn't grow on trees, but if we can teach our kids to be diligent with the resources that come their way, they will see the path on which they can make their own.

CHAPTER EIGHT

SIBLING RIVALRY, HONOR, AND RESPECT

If you are familiar with the movie *Ever After*, you will remember the scene in which the sisters chase each other through the house, screaming, pulling hair, and throwing shoes. We laugh at this now because although Jasmine didn't have a sister, she and Caleb played that scene out multiple times. Jasmine's personality was a copy of mine, and Caleb was his father to a tee, and these personality attributes were blazing examples of what we were before our years of refinement. Jasmine and Caleb were arch enemies! This is where the Wolfe Pack started, on the battlefield of intense sibling rivalry.

I am happy to say that through a lot of prayer, wisdom, and work, these two became best friends. The first signs of this shift came in their early teens. Even though there was still conflict at home, they were inseparable and insanely committed to each other's well-being during each church camp they attended. People at church would remark about how much they loved each other, and I would smile and nod on the outside while completely confused on the inside! By the time they hit high school, their relationship became authentic even at home.

I was so grateful because in those early years, I was sure we were in for a disaster. It was so important to me that our family become a place of love and strength for all members involved that I became very tenacious in my quest for familial love and unity. If you feel the same way, then you are desiring a very good thing. My encouragement to you would be to not give up. Everything in society today screams relational anger, division, and self-seeking. With loving determination from you as parents, you can direct your family toward love, unity, and selflessness. The path that leads you there is learning the way of honor and respect.

Sibling strife can be so disheartening and destructive. I know firsthand how absolutely helpless it can make us feel as parents. This chapter is designed to give you hope and very real, practical tools to tame those sibling tiffs.

Every family has a certain level of dysfunction in their relationships. Family can be the source of the deepest kind of pain. Yet family can also be the very lifeblood that sees us through the worst that life can dish out. It has deep levels of connection that can't be bought or replicated. It takes work to make family what it is intended to be. Every member must become selfless, patient, kind, loving, and self-controlled. Kind of sounds a bit like what Paul describes as the fruits of the Spirit, doesn't it?[39] In other words, for family to function well, it requires each individual to be like Christ, regardless of how un-Christlike anyone else is.

I was quite the caboose in my family, born nine years after my closest sibling and seventeen years after my oldest sibling. My oldest sibling was more of a father figure to me, since our father passed away just before I was born. The ensuing years presented a lot of challenges as we navigated life. It wasn't easy, and our sibling relationships remain a bit difficult to this day. Because of the tension, I was determined that my own family would function differently. I wanted my kids to love each other. As each child was born, it became more apparent that this would not be an easy task.

One day, I went shopping and bought a husband. Well, not literally, but we all go searching for our mate, in a sense. Most of us fall in love and marry the person of our choice. But please keep in mind that even when we get to choose, it is still very hard to continue to love, honor, and respect our spouse. As the years pass, we become more aware of our spouse's faults and frailties and more adept at criticism and negativity. Though we may love our spouse, honor and respect is always a choice that we must make.

Our children, on the other hand, never have the opportunity to pick their siblings. They never go through the falling-in-love, romantic, happy, giddy stage with each other. They don't have the benefit of deciding to declare, "I want to spend the rest of my life with you." They aren't allowed to stand at the altar and vow their lifelong dedication to the well-being of their sibling as you did with your spouse. Nope! Instead, they meet each other at the most selfish, most demanding, rudest, most unrefined times in each of their lives, and they are stuck with each other. Forgiveness, patience, honor, and respect are the order of the day and the exact opposite of what they want to do. Those of you who find yourselves in blended families, your children now find themselves thrown into very close quarters with other selfish, demanding, rude, and unrefined beings who don't even share the same DNA.

Raising children who honor, respect, and eventually love each other is nothing short of miraculous. Yet I want to encourage you as parents—it is possible!

Most of my kids are imperative, demanding leaders in their own way, and they did not appreciate submitting to anyone, especially their siblings. Dwain and I are polar opposites, and had we met as children, I think we would have completely annoyed each other. Our maturity as adults caused us to love the very things that were different and find completion in each other. Our kids each reflected one of us in our drastically different personalities, yet they did not have the opportunity (or ability) to say, "Wow, I love that you are not like me, and I really need you to help complete me as a whole person." Nope. It was total frustration, button pushing, anger, disdain, and downright meanness.

I am happy, blessed, and relieved that the Wolfe cubs all love each other dearly at this point. I cannot take all the credit for our situation, but I can share the things we did.

Some will work for you, and some won't. You will need to find the God-given keys for your children's hearts and use them effectively.

1. Pray.

A lot. You are going to need it. A lot of influences are set to cause your family to implode. It seems that there is a battle against both your marriage and your children, and a battle implies there is an enemy who wants to destroy— Satan. If the enemy of your family can't get you and your spouse to fight and hate each other, he will get your kids to. It's his intention to breed hatred and animosity anywhere he can. You need everything on your side to fight this war, including God. Get your strength and confidence in prayer, then go for the win in your day-to-day life.

2. Determine what peace looks like to you.

Some of us come from families who were constantly in strife and turmoil. You may not have a clue what it is like to live in peace or what it takes to get there. Begin to construct a vision of what a peaceful, loving household looks like. Look around you at families who may not be perfect but are doing a pretty good job. Spend time around them, taking note of what it feels like and learning how they relate to each other. Begin to assemble the things you observe as requirements of a peaceable home—things like forgiveness, selflessness, overlooking faults that need to be overlooked, and lovingly but constructively confronting what needs to change. Once again, it all starts with you, the parents. Practice these things with your spouse. Become very adept in honor and respect. We all must sow and grow peaceableness before we can reap peace.[40]

3. Allow for self-advocating, but don't allow tattling.

Your children are human and full of selfish ambition. They will want to harm others to benefit themselves. Tattling is reporting truth or even trumped-up charges to enjoy the ensuing repercussions. Self-advocating is seeking justice and protection against an aggressor. You will have to become adept at knowing the difference and how to react to both.

When my children fought, they always came to me with accusations against the other while playing the complete victim. Each had their own rendition of the incident, of course. It was very frustrating to me to constantly be playing judge and jury, presiding over these ruthless little prosecuting attorneys all day long, and I didn't always do it well. Over time, I learned to respond peaceably instead of with my own frustration, which helped immensely! As I got better at it, I came up with the following strategy.

The first thing I would do was stop the yelling. Next came the court scene, but instead of letting them proceed as prosecuting attorneys, I pulled a fast one. I only allowed each one to tell me everything that *they personally did wrong* in this situation. Now, instead of accusing the other of misdeeds, they were taking responsibility for their poor actions. It completely changed the situation. I encouraged them to tell the full story because after they were finished, the other was given the opportunity to fill in any details that were left out. By the time we were done, they were a bit more humble and ready to apologize. What would happen if our actual courts adopted this strategy?

Our family verse was Romans 12:18, New Mom Version: "Do everything in your power to be at peace with those around you." Everyone had to memorize it. If they couldn't think of anything they did wrong (hitting, kicking, name-calling, etc.), then I would ask them if they could think of anything they could have done better to be at peace with their brother or sister. Once again, if they were honest, there were always things they could have done, and they would slowly begin to admit them. This was a great way for me to teach my kids to take responsibility for their own choices and to end the victim mentality regarding behavior. We insisted on finding ways to do everything possible to be peaceable, instead of justifying defensive, reactive behavior because they were mad.

4. Constantly discuss honor and respect.

We can't make our children love each other; honor and respect, however, are choices and actions, not feelings. In a culture of honor and respect, love can grow. Require your kids to honor and respect one another through the common courtesies (that are not so common any more) of empathy and servanthood. Discipline disrespect. Continue to emphasize the uniqueness and dignity of each individual of your family as well as your family as a whole. In doing so, you set up the framework for honoring and respecting each other. Honor and respect are not given because someone is perfect; they're given because each family member is uniquely irreplaceable and important in his or her own way. If we were to lose any one of them (as sometimes a sibling may wish), the family would never be the same.

Sometimes a particular child can be annoying to another, either on purpose or otherwise. Either way, it causes those around him or her to feel disrespected and completely free to return the favor. This is where we as parents must be quick to draw the line on unacceptable behavior before others feel disrespected. If the behavior is on purpose, call it out and require the opposite. If the behavior is more of a result of annoying personality traits, then we need to get busy training this child in more socially acceptable habits. Children are masters at socially unacceptable quirks. One of mine hated to blow his nose, so he would constantly sniff; another one constantly had food all over his face during meals; and one left-handed child at the table constantly elbowed the others. All of these resulted in frustrated annoyance and required patient diligence from us as parents to resolve.

Sometimes one child can seem to struggle with respecting the others no matter the situation. This child quite often has difficulty locating compassion for those around him, so it's hard for him to care about how his sarcastic words or uncaring attitude affects others. Our challenge as parents is to develop this child's compassion for people and help him identify with how he makes people feel. When he is able to empathize, then he will be able to bridle his mean tendencies with honor and respect. Your first reaction with this child will probably be time-outs and separation from the rest of the family—and rightly so, because his behavior is hurtful. But at the same time, the family will need to work extra hard to pull him in and honor him for being a part, while still requiring honor from him for others. Find and celebrate his goodness, and it will help him begin to find goodness worthy of honor in others.

Once while Caleb was spending the night at a friend's house, Jasmine and I were outside his room and I made the comment that I missed him. Jasmine shot back very bluntly that she did *not* miss him. I went on to describe all the things that were lacking in our home without him. She listened and eventually began to join me in adding to the list.

TOP TIP #8

Respect and honor are two character traits that can grant your children the grace they need to enter the real world of business and relationships.

Because I didn't let the dishonoring of another remain unanswered, Jasmine responded by turning her heart toward honoring Caleb. Use your influence to turn the tide of negativity in your home at every opportunity.

5. Don't expect adult relationships from children.

Sometimes our expectations of our young children are too high. We envision perfectly loving interactions at all times. Reality is our constant reminder that we are dealing with the immaturity of our humanness. It causes us to give up out of hopelessness or get exasperated and join in their tirades. Remember that they are children who are susceptible to all sorts of selfishness—and they can be very creative in their delivery. Children are inherently self-centered. Everything is about their advancement and another's demise. Your job is to bend, mold, and prune. It's not an easy task if your child is made of the kind of grit and determination that can change the world—but it's necessary nonetheless—you are saving the world from being ruled by a tyrant! Consistency, faith, strength, and endurance will win the day, so don't lose sight of the prize. My kids were a rough lot in those early years. We all laugh now at their antics, but I can safely say they are now each other's favorite people. Keep your aspirations high and your daily reality filled with strong determination so that your family will yield to the things that produce great relationships.

6. Play the resident counselor.

At times in the teen to young-adult years, our children have had to reevaluate perceptions of their childhood interactions, maturing the viewpoints they had held throughout their early lives. Through simple but profound conversations about these events, they have been liberated from years of possible bitterness.

At times at our house, a certain child would become a bit vulnerable to me or my husband about how their relationship with a certain sibling was affected by their difficulties in the past. One time a certain cub had been deeply hurt by his sister's constant and harsh "bossing him around." Years later, I was able to help him see that she had found herself at the time in a place of authority by sheer birth order and was inexperienced, to say the least. It also helped him to remember that in those days, he needed correction to save the situation from spiraling out of control. As my cub began to understand the situation from a more mature perspective, he was able to let go of his bitterness and forgive her. This may sound like an innocuous situation, but it's things like this that, unresolved, can grow into lifelong vendettas.

Don't be too quick to make an appointment with the family counselor if you can help it. Instead, watch and listen for sensitive moments when you can help your children see things from a better perspective. You might be amazed at how viewpoints can change. However, if your family has gone through some rough years and there seems to be some residual animosity, by all means, consider seeking the help of professional counselors. It's important to do what it takes to bring peace and understanding so your family can move into the future with strong and vibrant relationships.

Conclusion

Honor and respect are desperately needed in today's society. Fight for peace in your home. As you do, you will find that your children will follow suit and become peaceful creatures themselves.

As you stand for honor and respect in your home, it's important to note how important manners are to your success. Manners are the beginning of our ability to put others first in our hearts and actions. The following chapter will help you in your quest to tame those crazy critters who live in your house!

CHAPTER NINE

MANNERS AND OTHER UNCOMMON COURTESIES

The other day, I was making small talk with a young man about the age of ten. He looked me in the eye and was very good at keeping up his side of the conversation, complete with "Mrs. Wolfe" and a healthy dose of "please" and "thank you." My immediate thought was *Good job, Mom and Dad!*

Though manners make humans successful, children do not come by them naturally. We as parents must model manners as we teach them. It's not always easy to keep our own bodily functions under control, let alone remember all the proper ways of doing things. Don't think for a minute it will be easy to get your little munchkins to abide by all of it either. If you want to instill manners in your child, don't be surprised if you feel like you are swimming upstream. In today's culture, you will definitely be attempting something that is not the norm. But believe me, it is well worth the struggle!

One of the parenting series we watched in those early VHS days at our church had an excellent portion on manners. Our church was small at the time, and just about all the parents went through the training. From my perspective, the children of New Horizon had the best manners around! It wasn't easy, but when we as parents made manners a priority, the results were wonderful.

Why are manners so important? In an increasingly child-centered world, manners are the things that cause our children to stop and consider others.

> Manners are interesting things. They are disarming, charming, but most of all, respectful. . . . We can only learn to respect ourselves through learning to respect others. Most people want to be respected and yet have not learned to be respectful. Being held in a position of respect can feed an ego, but the humility and grace learned through being respectful feeds a soul.[41]

Manners show respect and appreciation. *From Innocence to Entitlement* states:

> People who are mannerly and appreciative are generous. They live from a position of abundance. When people feel abundant, they see more possibilities and opportunities in their lives. Therefore, they are happier.[42]

Wow, all that from learning manners? I believe it, and

I believe the first place to start is with you as parents! If manners are not your forte, I urge you to get a book on teaching manners to your kids and read it yourself first. When I began to implement manners, I was challenged in my own daily life to address people with more respect and to act with better self-control.

There are many different areas of manners out there, and I did not insist on perfect etiquette, but the Wolfe Pack did do fairly well. The following are some of the things we insisted upon in daily life.

1. Please and thank you

Yes, you would think this is a no-brainer, but there are many out there who don't feel it's necessary. I work at our church's community outreaches, which quite often include giving children candy and small trinkets. I can honestly say that over half the children do not say either please or thank you. Instead, they often take as if they were owed the item and we were finally delivering. These small words are the beginning of teaching gratitude, and gratitude is the number one antidote to entitlement.

As another way to instill gratitude as a manner, I required my children to write thank-you notes to anyone who ever gave them a gift, especially if the giver was an adult. At Christmastime, after birthdays, and at any other time when they received gifts, my children returned their gratitude with a handwritten note. I received a thank-you note from a nephew this past Christmas, and I was so excited and impressed! I will admit, my children were never in the mood to write their thank-yous. When they complained, I would calmly tell them that if writing their thank-you note was too much to expect of them, we would simply need to return the gift—then they immediately found themselves in the mood!

2. Addressing adults as Mr. and Mrs.

Being the pastors of a church, our children had a lot of interaction with other adults, both close family friends and acquaintances. We made it a general rule that adults would be called by Miss, Mr., or Mrs. So-and-so, regardless of our relationship. I can't tell you how much this improved my children's level of respect and honor for those older than themselves.

Sometimes the adults they were addressing would be uncomfortable with the formality of the title. They would invite my children to call them by their first name. This is a kind gesture to imply a closer relationship. I then encouraged my children to call them Miss (first name) or Mr. (first name). This satisfied my desire to retain a bit of respect and yet allowed for a more intimate relationship.

3. Introductions and small talk

The Wolfe cubs became very adept at introductions— there were a lot of them at church! Teach your children to look the other person in the eye, shake their hand properly, answer questions such as, "How are you?" and then ask the questions in return. The ability to make small talk is very important as they become adults. It might even be what helps them access favor with a boss, client, etc. Teach your child that she needs to be interested in finding out about those around her and that she cannot just talk about herself.

Before I go any further, I know some of you are immediately concerned with our children's need to be aware of stranger danger. While our children were young, Dwain and I tried to instill in them the wisdom and knowledge that not all strangers are safe. We taught our children to be discerning as well as polite. I understand there is a fine line in determining when your child needs to engage in conversation and when it is unwise. Teach your children about these different circumstances and give them one-liners to avoid conversation. Your child might say, "I'm sorry, but I am waiting for my mother," or "Let me get my (parent, teacher, etc.)," and then go to an authority for safety. There are many ways to navigate the safety issue while still encouraging proper communication when things are safe.

Some children are shy and do not want to respond to adults when addressed. Teach your children the importance of a proper response and give them the confidence to look adults in the eye and respond appropriately. Begin with those they know and feel safe with. Practice ahead of time, introducing them to your spouse or to their siblings so they can understand the expectations and feel success. Shyness is generally not an excuse; they need to learn to overcome their fear.[43] If children are allowed to remain in their small-people world without being required to stop and interact with the adult-people world, they will not develop the security it takes to step out later in life. Help your child be confident and secure in interacting with all generations.

In the current world of screens and social media, the fine art of communication in person is becoming rare. Put away your screens and require the young ones to do the same. Spend your family time engaging and practicing good social interaction. Someday when they are out in the great big world, they will stand out in the crowd as young men or women who can engage with their boss, coworkers, and clients much better than others their age. As my children have found, this can be the very thing that lands them that job or that promotion.

4. Friends' houses

We taught our children that when they arrived at someone's home, they should always approach the parents of the home they were visiting to say hello. When they left, they were expected to thank the parents. We also taught our kids to take their shoes off at the door, regardless of that home's rules.

As your children implement these manners, you will see that they quickly become those parents' favorites! My children have developed great relationships with their friends' parents. I believe their manners made the parents feel respected and even caused them to appreciate my children's influence on their own children. Down through the years, my children have had opportunities to earn money through house-sitting and other arrangements as well as go on family vacations with them to places we would never have been able to take them! It pays in many ways to be polite, honoring, and respectful.

5. Opening doors, giving up seats, and honoring their elders

Dwain and I taught our children to open doors for others, give up their seats for adults, and, when appropriate, engage in conversation with them.

We required our children to walk their elderly grandmother out to the car and to offer her their arm as they went. This helped teach our children respect and honor for earlier generations and compassion for the elderly. If you don't have grandparents nearby, be intentional about putting your children in situations with older generations. Help your children hear and feel their place in life and how to treat them accordingly.

6. Noisy bodily functions

We did not allow our children to intentionally make noisy bodily functions. Raising three boys, it was plain to see this was going to be a challenge, but I found that girls can be just as bad! Noisy bodily functions were allowed on their beds and in the bathroom or if they were with *only* their friends. If an adult was present, they were to show respect and refrain.

You may think I am a bit old-fashioned, but I think it is important to teach our sons how to treat a female with extra respect in this arena. I wanted to raise gentlemen who knew how to treat ladies, and this was a great place to start.

We began with a conversation about the reality of flatulence and the need to honor and respect others by not subjecting them to your "situation." It was always approached with a lot of fun, yet I did mean business.

I enforced my edict with monetary requirements: a quarter for average noises and up to a dollar or two for the really big ones. I was even known to send the neighborhood children home for quarters! It worked great when they were young. As they grew older, the need for payment seemed to diminish as better habits formed. I will say that there did come a time when I put out my hand demanding payment and it was met instead with a laugh and, "I'm sorry, Mom, won't happen again." Apparently they were too old to fall for my gimmick, but the behavior change had taken place.

7. Language

We considered rude language off limits. My children were not allowed to say, "shut up," "stupid," or any other form of offensive language. The book of Ephesians says, "Do not let any unwholesome talk come out of your mouths," "nor should there be obscenity, foolish talk or coarse joking."[44] You as parents can take a look at these and other scriptures and tailor your home's conversation. Don't let society dictate what's acceptable language in your home. You are in charge.

8. Table manners

We worked hard to train our kids in the basics of table manners. I am sure we could have done better. My driving motivation was to require good-enough manners that someday when they were on a date or with someone of great importance, their inherent normal behavior would be perfectly acceptable. This would include chewing with their mouths closed; elbows off the table; not reaching or grabbing; and saying, "Please pass the . . .," etc. At times we would do a little more formal meal (holidays and such), and I would use these times to teach a few more bits of etiquette. As stated in an earlier chapter, we always required them to thank the cook and ask to be excused.

We did not allow our children to call food "gross." This saved us multiple times as we were at people's homes for dinner; instead of a child embarrassing Dwain and me by blurting out, "Ew, yuck," or "I don't like this! It's gross!" they would politely say, "This isn't my favorite." We were then able to take care of the situation appropriately without disrespecting the cook. Find your own polite way for your children to indicate their dislike while continuing to honor your hosts.

9. Interrupting

Kids want to be heard, and they want to be heard *now*. There is nothing more irritating than a child who interrupts her parents when they are talking to others. Though children are needy, they must learn patience and self-control.

When my kids were old enough, I taught them that if they verbally interrupted me, the answer was always going to be no. They could gently place a hand on my arm to let me know they needed something. I would then put my hand on theirs to acknowledge their need and that I would get to them as soon as the conversation allowed. I would then excuse myself and give the child the opportunity to speak. This taught them patience as well as respect for the conversation I was in.

Conclusion

Manners are more than just the niceties of life; they are the currency with which we pay respect and honor to others. Manners cause us to step out of selfishness and step into concern for others. Manners teach us to use self-control for the benefit of others. Research manners and see if there are a few that you could add to the list.

TOP TIP #9

Helping your children develop manners will coax them out of selfishness into consideration for others—truly a wondrous transformation.

I have a suspicion that some of you may be reading this and feeling like this might be a tough area for you. Maybe for one reason or another, teaching manners has not been a strong point in your family. Possibly you weren't taught manners, your spouse is not a practicing-manners person, or your offspring have just not cooperated. I hope you will take this section and seriously consider it. What are some things that you yourself can improve on and encourage your family in? If you are feeling overwhelmed, my suggestion is always to eat the elephant one bite at a time—using your manners, of course! Try one thing at a time and before you know it, you will have a family who honors one another through their common courtesies, and that huge, formidable monster called disrespect will be taken down just a bit more!

Raising kids with thoughtful consideration benefits not just them and your immediate family—all society will join me in thanking you!

CHAPTER TEN

THE BIRDS AND THE BEES: DATING AND BEYOND

It all happens faster than you could imagine!

I had all the Wolfe cubs at the beach one sunny summer day. A busload of day-care children piled out of the bus and onto the beach. I was trying to read my book, visit with my friend, and keep my eye on all the yelling, splashing kids in front of me. At one point, I saw a little girl approach my kindergarten-aged third born, tell him he was cute, and ask for his phone number. I was there in a flash, stepping between them with hands on my hips, demanding to know where her mother was. She pointed to the sixteen-year-old day-care worker—I couldn't exactly complain to him! I told the girl to leave my son alone and go play somewhere else. I knew my boys were exceptionally handsome, but this was ridiculous. I was the one he was going to marry—he had told me so just that morning!

The *talk*. Dating. Sexuality. Just the words can make a good parent tremble.

Dwain and I always said, "No dating until you are sixteen." I'm not sure where sixteen came from, but it seemed we had plenty of time. All was well until my fifteen-year-old, ninth-grade firstborn started high school. When I was growing up, high school started in tenth grade, so this was new to me. Lots of things were changing, and it all was coming so fast—attitudes, new friends I didn't know, varsity cheer squad, and *boys*!

One Friday night, the Wolfe Pack was in the family van coming home from a church event when Jasmine announced she was going to "hang out" with some friends. We were okay with that, since she was going with a girl we knew and "a few other kids." When we pulled up, there was a car on the curb with two boys and her one girlfriend. We quickly realized this was not a hangout. It was a *date*! A double date at fifteen! We had about ten seconds to communicate before she jumped out of our car and into theirs. We had quite a conversation when she returned home, though she was adamant it wasn't a date, just a hangout. (By her standards, she never once had a date—it was always just "hanging out.")

Let me repeat: it happens way too fast! Our problem was that we didn't realize how early we needed to be prepared. We should have been discussing the topic more extensively from an early age, but because we thought we had plenty of time, we hadn't completely prepared our daughter for this season. And now here we were, scrambling a bit with a very smart fifteen-year-old and some feeble rules based on our own upbringing.

Dwain and I quickly started seeking out all the wisdom and advice we could find, doing our best to synthesize it into everyday life. By the grace of God, I think it's safe to say the Wolfe Den navigated these waters successfully. Here are some pointers from how we handled sexuality and relationships, along with a few ideas of things we *wish* we had done.

1. Start early.

It's never too soon—or too late, for that matter—to get wisdom and direction through great books and from those around you who have done well in the arena of healthy sexuality with their kids. Take some time to ask parents of older children how they approached this subject. Some may likely attribute their success to luck, but others just might have some great ideas.

When I say start early, I mean early. In their book *A Chicken's Guide to Talking Turkey with Your Kids about Sex*, Dr. Kevin Leman and Kathy Flores Bell say that parental influence on children's sexuality and relationships begins on the changing table. All *your* attitudes about sexuality, the opposite sex, relationships, and the like, be they positive or negative, are passed on to your children, starting from birth. Imprinting healthy sexuality into our children is more than a few "talks"—it's modeling how to be healthy in every one of these aspects.[45] For example, how you communicate with your spouse will convey either respect or disdain for the opposite sex. This attitude will shape your child's perspective, for better or worse.

If you are concerned that your mind-set toward sexuality has not been the healthiest, see this as a great (and extremely important) opportunity for you as the parent to grow, change, and become healthier in your own world. Remember, parenting challenges us as parents to first walk well in the very things we want for our children.

I highly recommend a couple great Christian children's books. Stan and Brenna Jones have a four-book series starting with three-year-olds and running through the teen years called God's Design for Sex. The book referenced above, *A Chicken's Guide to Talking Turkey with Your Kids about Sex*, is fantastic to read for some great ideas and to stock up on all the ammo you can. Anything that gets open, clear, comfortable conversation will make a big difference. It's never too early for you to consider what your attitude and approach will be toward educating your children in sexuality. Finding resources such as these books can help your planning and ease the conversations. Your precious little ones will very soon enter this realm, and you want to

TOP TIP #10

Talk about sexuality early and establish bonds of trust with your children. You are their main source for truth, so don't leave this to others!

be the first to take them there—not the neighborhood kids! Establish the communication pathways early and travel them often enough to keep them open so awkwardness does not intervene.

On a practical note, it's good to establish proper names for your children's body parts very early on, before you add in the more lighthearted names. This way you can have a very straightforward approach as to what is off-limits, and if there is ever any inappropriate touch or sexual abuse, you *and* your child can have a clear, concise conversation as to what actually happened.

Both parents play a vital role in guiding children toward healthy sexuality during the early years. It's good to note that the same-sex parent shares a familiar connection to his or her child's feelings and situations. Mothers help their daughters and fathers help their sons with positive understanding and with the how-tos of their sexual identity. The opposite-sex parent helps the child understand how the "other side" perceives things, which is quite often very different from how they might naturally think. For example, I had great (and at times quite funny) conversations with my sons about how girls think, beginning around this time and continuing into the teen years.

As your kids grow up, it's good for opposite-sex parents to begin taking their kids on dates. Mother-son and daddy-daughter dates are perfect times to shape role identity, manners, and positive self-image. At younger ages, you can emphasize dressing up for the date—make it extra special before they get too cool! We did this to some extent, but not nearly enough.

Have fun, especially in encouraging your same-sex child. If you establish your favorite mother-daughter and father-son activities early on, you will be more likely to share a connection that will help you ride out the preteen retreat into awkward embarrassment.

2. Around middle elementary school, start talking about what your children like and don't like about the opposite sex.

We found at the Wolfe Den that all four cubs were uncomfortable talking about sexuality (this was probably a result of a scarring attempt to teach the basics of reproduction with pet bunnies). Our first three cubs felt awkward talking about romantic relationships at all. It was harder to communicate about this area of their lives than almost any other, although, thankfully, the fourth cub was more open to sharing about his crushes. Despite the difficulty, we continued to wade into the subject of sexuality with each of our children with a loving, lighthearted, yet truth-filled approach—whether or not we were welcomed. This made way for eventual conversations that proved to be pivotal.

It's important for us as parents to establish comfortable openness regarding sexuality, romantic love, relationships, and marriage. Free and open communication regarding sexuality and relationships positions you—not a friend or a teacher—as the one who gives your child his first exposure to these concepts. You are placing yourself in the role of coach rather than warden. Every child is different; nonetheless, start early and be willing to venture where angels fear to tread.

As your children come to the beginning of puberty, things start getting fun! Communication about sexuality and the opposite sex begins to increase, and rightly so. By this time, parents can be enjoying the good highway of open communication that they began in the earlier years. This is a great time to be asking if there are any cuties at school who catch your child's eye or if anyone at school is going out with anyone else. In the Wolfe Den, we approached these conversations with great fun, just to get our cubs talking, not to encourage them to become girl or boy crazy; we wanted to begin having conversations concerning their hearts and minds regarding relationships.

In these early conversations, Dwain and I also asked our children questions about what they liked in the opposite sex, such as what made them interested in certain individuals they seemed keen on. It's good to get them thinking about their values when it comes to crushes. Eventually, these conversations led to similar discussions in young adulthood as they considered potential spouses. Children will automatically retreat into themselves when it comes to "romance." But when the conversational path is well worn, it becomes more comfortable as they get older and the stakes get higher.

3. Go to your children's school information night to see what their sex ed will be like.

While some begin sexuality training as early as kindergarten, schools generally hold formal sex education in middle elementary. Find out what information your kids will hear and how it will be presented at their school. That way you can make an informed decision on your child's participation and consider any corrections you want to make.

If you're worried about your child's exposure to sex education and are considering homeschooling or sending your children to a private school, take the time to visit the principal at your local public school. Get a feel for his or her philosophy on education, sexuality, and whatever else is valuable to you. The more you know about your local school, the more your choice will be a fully informed one instead of one based on fear. The Wolfe cubs started out in a wonderful private school, but to be honest, we chose it partially out of fear of where public education and sexuality training were heading. The financial burden began to increase and I started to realize that I was missing out on community involvement, so I made an appointment with the principal at our local elementary school. I was pleasantly surprised to find our principal was a former children's pastor! My children's school was overseen by someone who carried my values and, in turn, valued my involvement.

Though the environment of public education can be challenging, there are wonderful teachers and faculty who need support. The most important thing in this decision is to do what is right for you and your children. Know that even if your choices are limited by finances or life situation, God is watching over your child, and your influence at home is more powerful than what your child gets at school. Explore all your possibilities so that instead of being driven by fear, you can be led by God to where your child—and you—can learn and influence others for the best.

Regardless of what school situation your children are in, you, the parent, are your children's first and most influential sex ed teacher. Dads should go through the book *Preparing Your Son for Every Man's Battle* with their sons in the mid- to late-elementary years. This book is an excellent guide for fathers as they engage their sons in meaningful conversation, and it works particularly well when used before the school's sex education begins or alongside homeschooling curriculum. The first half contains information and encouragement for dads as they venture into shaping their sons' sexuality; the second half is a workbook guide to go through with sons. Dwain went through these books with each of the boys individually. Typically, he would set up a campout in their rooms (blankets for both of them on the floor) and he would read to them and tell them stories of his own. It wasn't always easy, and certain cubs sometimes chafed at it, but it ultimately established healthy views of sexuality in our sons.

Moms, you are not off the hook! Take your daughter out for something special and have a chat as you go. You may also want to look at Shannon Ethridge's *Preparing Your Daughter for Every Woman's Battle*.

If you are a single parent, ask your pastor, your children's youth pastor, or even a close, trustworthy friend to help take your son or daughter through the appropriate book. God can meet you in your need and cover your situation. Seek out support and watch God be the Father to the fatherless (and a mother to the motherless). He is able to provide what is needed in every situation, including yours. Take Him at His word and rest in His promises.

As you have conversations with your children, embrace their questions and help them understand the things they are thinking and feeling. Be there in the middle of their confusion to help them find truth. Always be seeking information if you don't know the answers. These kids are pretty good at throwing curveballs, and now is not the time to start breaking a sweat!

4. Establish rites of passage.

While establishing rites of passage will benefit your children through their entire lives, it becomes especially important during the teen years. Planning special events and rituals will not only guide your child toward healthy sexuality but also help guide them from childhood into adulthood. The Wolfe Pack was a bit in the dark on this, but I want to encourage you to take a better route. In generations past, there were definite markers as to when a child was passing into adulthood. It was a sign for both the child and the adults around him that his life as a child was coming to a close and he now had greater expectations and benefits. Without these defined markers, we are seeing young adults remain in adolescence well into their twenties.[46]

Mark specific birthdays for both sons and daughters with an activity and a change in their life. You can determine what birthdays are significant, but the transition at thirteen is a great place to start, if you haven't already.

This marks your child's stepping out of childhood and into the teen years, which are accompanied with added privileges and responsibility. A milestone for the Wolfe Pack was the sixteenth birthday. We would have a special party, and I would also take them into the bank to open checking accounts, complete with debit cards for them to manage their own money. The Wolfe cubs saw this as an incredible vote of confidence and relished the beginning of their financial independence.

Another important passage is your daughter's first menstrual cycle. Make it a precious time by taking her out for a special date or a shopping trip for something that would signify her growing up. Or if you can, take her on a special trip with just the two of you. In any case, allow for time to talk about sexuality and her coming menses, preparing her with the needed supplies so there isn't a mad dash or possible embarrassment. As girls continue to mature, it is also important for fathers to validate their daughters with dates and other ways of affirming their femininity.

Sons don't have a very strong marker that they are maturing into manhood; therefore, we need to create them. In times past and in other cultures today, men might take a boy out to accomplish something difficult. When they returned, the boy was viewed no longer as a child, but as a man. This is something we can do as well. You could take your son on a hike or adventure that challenges him and allows him to feel the thrill of overcoming something bigger than himself. Be creative in making a rite of passage that works for your family. As the young man returns to family life, be sure there is a shift of privilege and responsibility as well as a change in the way you engage him. He is growing up, and both mom and dad need to validate that fact.

When my sons were approaching high school graduation, I had some purposeful conversations with them in which I curtailed my mothering and spoke to them as adults. I felt it was important to express how I saw them as men and how I respected them as such. In the same way, I can't express how important it is for fathers to declare their approval of their sons' manhood. Likewise, both parents need to express their unconditional love for their daughters as women. This is a time for team effort.

5. Discuss your children's possible relationships before they happen.

The teen years mark the pursuit of opposite-sex relationships in a more serious manner. When our kids were teenagers, the in thing among our church circles was to not date at all. The book *I Kissed Dating Goodbye* had just come out, and it supported the no-dating policy until you found the person you wanted to marry. I knew families who had adopted this approach, and their kids seemed to be on board. Taking a no-dating stance can protect teens' hearts, bodies, and futures. It sounds good on paper, but my kids didn't buy in. And that's the thing—your kids have to buy in. This is not something I suggest you insist upon. Unless it becomes the teen's idea, it will only incite rebellion and animosity between her and her parents.

Instead of the no-dating policy, we chose to follow the advice given in *Boundaries in Dating* by Henry Cloud and John Townsend. This book encouraged us to allow the dating process to happen, but with well-designed boundaries and with us parents in the coaching role. Our teens will be in relationships whether we like it or not. They will begin separating from us and committing the better part of their lives to another person. We wanted to be in the middle of that process, helping them determine personalities, understand relational nuances, and process disappointments.

It's important to keep placing ourselves in the middle of these conversations with our teens as much as they will allow. Starting the summer before their eighth- or ninth-grade year (depending on their maturity), we sat down with each cub and talked about the possibility of relationships happening that year. We ended the time by having them write out what they felt were appropriate boundaries and rules with the opposite sex for that year. It was great because they were making their own rules—and they were usually harder on themselves than I would have been. We would hang the rules up in their room for the duration of that year. Then, if they happened to find themselves in a relationship, we could remind them of their own rules. This worked much better than trying to talk about boundaries when they were in the heat of a romantic relationship. We would rework their personal boundaries as time went on, but we always did this before it became an issue.

As your teens begin to approach those dating years, it's good to encourage them to read a book on dating—or better yet, read it with them. New books are always being written, so find the latest and greatest and encourage your teen to dive in. It's best to do this before your teens find themselves in the middle of a relationship so you don't end up in a power struggle. You'll also be prepared with relevant discussion topics once a relationship does start.

6. As your teens engage in the dating process, stay close.

When your teen begins to enter into a relationship, keep an open line of communication as much as possible. Ask her what she sees in that person that is good as well as what she might see as troubling. If a long-term relationship begins to materialize, meet the boyfriend's parents and invite them over for dinner. Talk about your boundaries and expectations, always doing so in an amiable, "cool" manner so your teen doesn't get too embarrassed. Be clear about guidelines while still accepting the relationship. If you are not happy about the relationship, let boundaries and consequences continue to rule the day. Talk, talk, talk your teen about your misgivings, yet love, love, love her. If you have done a good job of creating a family culture that she values, she will have that pulling on her, keeping her from separating from you for the boyfriend.

Being the great (a nice term for maybe a bit controlling and possibly overbearing) mom that I am, I found myself in that awkward place in which my college-graduate children were dating while they were in another state. I did not have the opportunity to meet the prospects or weigh in with my incredible advice. I was forced to take a deep breath, step back, and rest in everything we had instilled in them. When you have done your best and the hands-on parenting time is done, rest in your good work and the fact that they are God's kids, and He will take it from there. Tell them how much you believe in their values and good character, then *pray like crazy*! It's all going to turn out for the best.

Sexual Identity

Before concluding this chapter, I want to cover one more important subject: sexual identity. I briefly touched on it earlier, but its importance merits more attention.

When we were raising our cubs, the topic of sexual identity was much more straightforward than it is today. Today, the gender lines have blurred, and many parents are worried and confused about how to teach their children in this important area. I hope to renew your confidence that male and female are, in fact, two very different things and that masculinity and femininity are natural, positive, and needed. I also hope to give you courage for navigating this subject with your children from a position of strength, confidence, and understanding. It's an extensive subject, so I encourage you to read more on the topic when you finish this book.[47]

In considering sexual identity, we must keep in mind that there is a difference between gender roles (things we do) and gender qualities (our essence). Roles are practical things, such as taking out the trash, fixing cars, cooking, and caring for children. Roles are "assigned" by need, gifting, and willingness to jump in; either male or female can do these things without a gender-identity crisis. However, sexual identity is about the innate essence that is within the genders, not whether a girl fixes cars or boys cook.

This essence, or identity, comes from God Himself. The Bible tells us, "So God created mankind in his own image, in the image of God he created them; male and female he created them."[48] God took His singular essence and separated it into two parts that are unique yet equal. Masculinity and femininity both carry a portion of God's essence.

Some of these masculine qualities are considered to be strength, courage, protection, dominance, risk-taking, competition, and provision. Some feminine qualities include beauty, caringness, empathy, community, gentleness, sensitivity, communicativeness, emotionality, and nurture.[49] This doesn't mean both genders can't possess or demonstrate any number of these qualities; it simply means a male will usually have a propensity to male qualities, and a female will tend toward the female qualities.

When our children are infants and toddlers, we place an emphasis on nurture and connection. As time goes on, we emphasize courage and bravery. The child is experiencing a mixture of both masculinity and femininity. This is good, because our girls need to be brave and our boys need to be emotionally intelligent.

But a time comes when children must begin to specialize in their identity. It's important that opposite-sex parents (mother/son and father/daughter) begin to provide loving yet intentional direction toward proper identity.[50] Mothers need to lovingly push their sons toward masculinity by respecting their courage and risk-taking as well as valuing their strength instead of sowing fear and ambivalence toward manhood. Dwain bought dirt bikes for the boys when they were young (Jasmine was not interested). During the many dad-and-sons motorbike trips, the boys took risks, challenged their fears, and came back to camp triumphant, all while I had to restrain my instinct to hold them back and protect them from potential danger. I cheered them on, applauding their accomplishments.

Similarly, fathers need to lovingly nudge their daughters toward femininity by valuing their beauty and nurturing connectedness with them instead of withdrawing from them at a time when interactions may become more awkward. As I took Jasmine to get makeup consultations and I attended dance and cheer clinics and competitions, her daddy cheered her on and affirmed her in all that she was becoming.

As the "nudging" opposite-sex parent respects and values the child's developing masculine or feminine traits that are opposite their own, the same-sex parent (mother/daughter and father/son) takes on the role of drawing the child toward his or her identity by welcoming the child into their world. Now is not the time for a mother to shame her daughter for her courage and risk-taking; instead, she should take these strengths into her feminine world and teach her how to clothe her beauty with strength and courage. This is not the time for fathers to shame a son for his sensitivity; instead, it is a time to teach him strength and boldness with a caring understanding.

Remember, the importance is not on activities or roles, but on essence and identity. The important part of Dwain's and my parenting wasn't teaching our man cubs how to ride motorbikes; it was fostering courage and risk-taking, and for my part, releasing them from my nurturing protection and my inclination toward the clean, neat, and orderly. This was essential in helping our sons become independent men unafraid to make their place in the world.

Do your sons have different interests than camping or motorbiking? Think about how you can help them take risks, overcome fears and difficulties, and leave the comfort of mom's side as they pursue those interests. Are shopping and makeup of little interest to your daughter? Then consider how you can celebrate her beauty, grace, and sensitivity in the areas that do interest her. How can you help her become a strong communicator, nurturer, and builder of community? How can you demonstrate to her the equal value she has as one created in God's image, giving her freedom to excel and lead others while celebrating her femininity?

I must take a moment to address those who are bravely raising their kids single-handedly. You are my hero! Guiding your son or daughter into healthy sexuality can seem like a daunting task without the other parent to help. I want to encourage you— you are up for it! You must play both parts by first valuing, honoring, and respecting the opposite-sex child and his or her journey toward something different from you. Secondly, you must provide a clear pathway into that masculinity or femininity in every way possible. This can be done by finding others around you to take your boy camping, shooting, car fixing, fishing, or anything else you believe might help him bond with other men and embrace his masculinity. And in the same way, you must encourage your daughter regarding things important to her femininity. I realize that some single moms are great at the camping/fishing/hunting thing and some single dads are great at shopping for pretty dresses and such. If that is the case, go for it! Otherwise, look to family members, church friends, and others who can be that role model. Just remember, your goal is to create a pathway for your son or daughter to become something different from you. They need to individuate toward masculinity and femininity, and that is not something they can actually pattern after you. Instead, you are needed to instill respect and value in their differences as well as to provide a defined pathway to get there.

Healthy sexuality is important for your child's success. As more research comes out and as more time passes, we will see that traditional viewpoints stand the test. However, our society is doing anything it can to tell us otherwise. I can't close this important section out without emphasizing the need to cover your children in prayer and seek God for direction for your individual child. In combining prayer and wisdom, you and your children will win.

Conclusion

Regardless of how old your children are, take time to read up on great ways to talk to them about sex and their sexuality as well as teen dating and relationships. Believe it or not, it's been a while since you were in their shoes, and as fast as society is moving, I highly recommend you get educated!

If you are further down the road of dating and sexuality with your teens and find them in less-than-ideal circumstances, my heart goes out to you. You may feel that you have lost your voice in their lives when the finish line is so close.

I want to encourage you to never stop speaking life and truth into your children's hearts, especially regarding their sexuality and relationships. Now is not the time to lose hope, get tired, and give up. Instead, take your young person to the throne room of grace as you pray earnestly for wisdom and direction. Culture screams a very different thing than traditional morality, and if you want to draw your child toward higher and better, you will need to be ready to stand until you see it come to pass. Once again, get your hands on every sound book pertaining to your situation. Talk to pastors and professionals who are familiar with what you are facing. Find those in your church who have dealt with similar situations and ask them for practical wisdom and a listening ear to help you stay the course.

As you communicate with your teen about his or her situation, you need to walk a fine line between love and honesty, because both are needed. You can't stop bringing wisdom, but it must be doused in unconditional love, so your child stays connected and open to your words.

Don't let go of those wonderful teens. Just this morning, Cub Number Four and I were reminiscing about some of the things we had gone through with him. He was seeing it from our side for the first time, and he was a bit apologetic. I told him that we as parents had been able to see all the potential in him and had been willing to stay in the ring with him because we loved him so deeply. The greatness within him was worth the extra effort.

There are times when we as parents get tired and are tempted to coast through this last lap of child raising, but this is not the time to rest—this is the time to ramp it up, kick it in gear, and see it to the end. Your teens are worth all the blood, sweat, and tears of the investment required to finish strong.

CHAPTER ELEVEN

INSTILLING FAITH

In this chapter, you will no doubt notice that I'm addressing my comments to Christian parents. If you aren't sure where you stand with the whole God and Christianity thing, I understand. I'd like to encourage you to think about your beliefs in this area once again. Everyone has a belief about God, you included. There is nothing in all the world that I would desire more than for you to believe that God loves you and wants to help you. I would love for you to come to a saving faith in Jesus and learn what it means to become more like Him. Christ was the best at loving people while calling them to higher and better things. He was also incredible at giving people purpose in their life's work. He is a great model for parenting. Truly, nothing will help you more in this parenting journey than to invite God into your family.

For those of you who have given your life to Christ, it is essential to pass on this valuable part of life to your children. Everything we truly believe comes out in word and deed. Yet I could place a safe bet that all of us fail at times in our word and deed. It's in our humble repentance as parents that we get to show the value of our loving heavenly Father. This grace and mercy is something that makes life, relationships, and family more than bearable—even enjoyable.

TOP TIP #11

Your children will blossom as they take up faith's mantle, becoming more Christlike on the inside rather than rules driven on the outside.

Passing your faith on to your children is the most important thing you can do for them. I believe it even trumps the goals of loving well and successful work! I have watched one generation shift the spiritual course from a long lineage of godliness to atheism within twenty years. In fact, it's been said that the outcome of a child is only 30 percent parental input, while 70 percent is the child's makeup and decisions.[51] It seems crazy that a book on parenting can only claim a 30 percent effectiveness, but that 30 percent can be incredibly powerful, especially when it comes to passing on our faith.

Our influence of faith in our children's lives is phenomenal. I have had the privilege of watching all four of the Wolfe cubs walk through their doubting teen years and then come to a personal decision to walk with Christ for themselves. The role Dwain and I had in their decision was very important. When you see your grown children finding churches on their own and becoming part of a community of believers, you can truly shout, "Yes!"

When your children choose to live for God, there is so much hope for them in every arena. They will have the teaching and understanding of how to love well. They will have great input in successful marriages. They will be challenged personally to live upright and above reproach. They will be encouraged to reach for their God-given destiny and work hard at it. All this and so much more will be available to them. Faith in God truly is an important part of maturation.

So, what can we do in our 30 percent influence to encourage faith in our children? While it's true that children learn more from modeling than from teaching, don't underestimate the power of teaching!

Following are a few ways you can pass on a strong faith to the younger generation.

1. Live well as parents.

Hypocrisy has no room in your home. Living by Christ's example is more powerful than a million sermons. Let your kids see you pray. Let your kids hear you discuss spiritual things. Let your kids see you walk full of integrity as you daily live out the Ten Commandments. Serve and have your kids serve with you. Take your kids on outreaches, feeding the hungry or sharing the gospel. Go on mission trips. Let them see you give financially to the church and give God the glory for miraculous provision. If your walk with the Lord is vibrant and alive, then your children will find it very natural to walk with the Lord as well. As I have mentioned before, parenting well demands that we as parents step up to the plate in every area, and this one is no exception.

Talk about the things in life that don't make sense. Talk about the concepts of trust and obedience. Let them see you struggle to forgive and then find peace and love for the offender. If you can do it, so can they! Take the needed time to stay on a strong growth curve yourself. Show your kids how covenant relationships lovingly confront and then fully forgive, from your spouse to your family, pastors, and friendships.

Do Christianity in your own daily life. In doing so, you will be filled with life and joy. Your kids will be likely to follow suit.

2. Make church a part of your family culture.

First and foremost, find a great church, one that you can really support and to which you feel the Lord has called you. Once you have settled in, buy in, dig in, and sign up! If you start your kids early, then it will be just a normal part of your life.

Sometimes church attendance can be seen as a burden—but it really isn't! Church is an amazing place that can be life-giving for every member of your family. Some families allow their kids to skip if they are bored or don't want to go. But I don't see church as the problem; it's more likely the children's attempt at controlling their world. We are the pastors of our church, so our kids had no choice but to attend church with a happy attitude. There were a few times when they complained, but we made it clear that it's just what we do. There wasn't too much pushback, because it was a nonnegotiable. We made it fun and a family project. Don't fall prey to the "I don't want to force them" routine. Why should church be an optional part of a child's life when school, chores, and eating broccoli aren't? Nope, at our house, going to church was what we did, and we loved it. My children are not bitter over it.

A side note to those with children entering the middle-school and teen years: these are very important years, and your kids must be involved in a good youth group. This is not the time to change churches or become too busy with activities. They need to be plugged in and attending everything possible. You will need other voices in your teen's life who say the same thing you are saying. Sometimes they will hear it better when it's coming from the cool youth leader!

3. Read the Bible with your kids.

Long ago, schools used the Bible as their primer to teach kids to read. Unfortunately, those days are gone. Unless your kids are enrolled in Christian school, they will only hear godly teaching at church on Sundays and from you.

When my children were in elementary school, I started to wake them up about twenty minutes earlier than needed.

(If you don't say a word, they won't know the difference!) They got dressed and I had breakfast ready. After they ate, we sat in the dining room on the heater vent with a big blanket. We all snuggled up while I read a chapter or two from the Bible. I stuck with the historical books while they were young. We would then each pray for someone in their class and for something each one needed. Then it was off to school. Unfortunately, I found that as they moved on to junior high and high school, the timing made it a bit more complicated, but we did the best we could. As the last child entered his last years of high school, our Bible reading became a precious part of our mornings. I also ventured out to Christian books such as *The Case for a Creator* by Lee Strobel and *Doubting* by Alister McGrath. We have had many meaningful discussions as a result.

Don't leave the spiritual training to the Sunday-school teacher. You are the best thing your kids have. And who knows, you might become a Bible scholar along the way!

4. Have family devotions.

When the kids were preschool and elementary-school age, there was a huge push in the Christian community to have family devotions. The idea was that the father would sit on the couch with all the children sitting around in rapt attention as he read from the Bible. Then, everyone would sing and love God with all their hearts.

We did our best to emulate this strategy every Tuesday evening. It never went quite as planned. The kids would usually start a pillow fight. Someone would pass gas or do something that would totally throw everything into disarray. It would end in frustration on our part and unceasing laughter on theirs. We then resorted to just singing fun songs and praying a bit. This went better (sort of). We now have lots of fun stories of Dwain with the guitar leading us all in old youth-ministry songs as we tried to teach our kids how to harmonize. It just never went the way we had intended, but we tried, and they didn't spend the night doing their own thing, so I'd call it a success.

Give something a try. Have fun with it. Turn off the TV, do *something* with your family spiritually, and see what godly bonding can do for your family.

5. Pray like crazy!

I can't promise that if you live like an amazing Christian, get your kids to church every week, read the Bible, and have family devotions, your children will all serve God. Remember that 70 percent? Yep, it's very much in play. Not to mention the fact that your children are targets of the enemy and that he would love to snatch them out from under your grasp. Pray for them.

We would go into our children's rooms at bedtime and pray with them. Then we would sneak back in after they were asleep and pray for them. We would pray together as parents, declaring the will of God over them. We prayed that they would never get away with anything. We prayed that they would be deathly allergic to drugs and alcohol (this actually came to pass!). We prayed love and life over them. And we continue to pray daily for them.[52]

Conclusion

Those moments when your children are transitioning into adulthood and the spiritual imprint from you and your household becomes apparent are worth more than you can imagine. Put in the effort and know that God's Word will never return void.

Before closing this section, I would like to pause and take a moment to address those parents who find themselves with children who are protesting participation in church and seem hard-hearted toward God. Every situation is unique and, unfortunately, the scope of this book does not allow me to address these situations specifically. Generally speaking, though, it is important to keep the focus on the main things. Each one of us has a God-given gift of free will, including your children. They can choose. We can't control them. It's our job to lead them to God, and it's their job to accept Him. I know it can be heartbreaking to watch the struggle and easy to fear the worst. Keep praying, believing, loving, and doing what you can to lead them into good places. Reach out to your pastor or youth pastor for support and guidance. Help your child find those who are willing to be a mentor.

For a season in my daughter's teen life, things became difficult on many fronts. She wouldn't listen to us, and both my husband and I knew she was wrestling with her beliefs and values. A young woman who was a youth leader at our church reached out and developed a relationship with Jasmine. They had coffee and hung out, all the while talking about the things that were troubling Jasmine. My heart rested safely in this relationship because I knew she was saying the same things I was saying, but with a different voice. I am certain this was pivotal in these years as Jasmine was making choices and developing thought patterns that are still with her today. I am so grateful that I had this backup.

Don't lose hope—it's not over yet!

Start children off on the way they should go, and even when they are old they will not turn from it.[53]

CHAPTER TWELVE

LET 'EM GO AND WATCH 'EM GROW

I loved being pregnant. I was extremely large and definitely in charge! Literally. During those nine-month spans, I was the closest I would ever be to my children. I felt their every move. We shared meals. I took them with me everywhere I went. But the moment they were born, the separation began.

The first night after Jasmine was born, the nurses took her to the nursery so I could get some rest. I fell right to sleep. Then I awakened in the middle of the night with a start—for the first time in her tiny life, I didn't know where she was. I jumped (as much as a postpartum mom could jump) out of bed and wandered the halls, asking if anyone knew where my baby was. I was pointed to the nursery. I will never forget the feeling I had as I came to the door and scanned the fifteen or so bassinets . . . *Where is my baby?* It was a mixture of fear, mama-bear instinct, and wondering, "What in the world am I doing?! I've been a mom for twelve hours and have already lost her!"

It seemed from that day forward Jasmine was on a mission to grow up. I would put her in the nursery at church and then sit through service, hoping her number would come up so I could save the day. It never did. She was having far too much fun on her own! With every new season, I went through another round of letting go. On the first day of junior high, I drove her to school and followed her in, determined to get those first-day-of-school pictures with friends and teachers, just like I had all through elementary school. She did her best to lose me in the sea of students. The first time she drove away with her newly acquired driver's license, I ran along the sidewalk, videotaping her all the way out of the neighborhood. The time we drove her across the country for her master's program in Washington, DC, I hugged her on the curb of her new apartment and then drove away bawling.

There has been a lot of letting go. You would think I would be a professional at it by now. Nope. As I face my last born starting college, I am once again faced with change and the challenge of letting go. I can't say it has become any easier since I started with the first cub; it's just a little different. I wish I could say I have been incredibly poised and full of amazing strength during all these changes. Nope. I was scared, sad, and emotional. But each time I would suck it up, smile, cheer each one on, and then go home, cry, and pray until it felt better. I could then face my new reality with courage and even a bit of excitement, knowing that each change was exactly what was right.

It's our children's job from birth to become independent and leave us. It's our job as parents to inspire them to become independent and leave us. Every step is poignant, challenging, and new. Neither of you have done this before.

Some parents can't wait for their children to grow up and leave home. These are the parents doing a happy dance on the first day of kindergarten. Others are grieving the loss of all things childhood, saving every lost tooth, every drawing, and every shred of their child's favorite blankie. Wherever you find yourself on the continuum, you must get good at both letting your child go and providing a comfortable, secure place where they can return to called home and family.

It's a fine line. Growing up too fast can be dangerous, but allowing children to linger in their childhood can be debilitating. We must become adept at providing security and expecting them to move on. We must know when to unfluff the nest, making the comforts of childhood a bit less comfortable so the little bird will take the leap and fly solo. As stated earlier, current research has shown that adolescence is extending farther and farther into a child's twenties.[54] While I'm sure there are many reasons for this new phenomenon, I think one reason could be that parents just don't want to let go.

Most children are a bit ambivalent as they cross into new seasons. One time when Jasmine was in fifth grade, I picked her up from staying the night with her friend. She seemed a bit different, a bit grown-up, sitting with her legs crossed, flipping her hair, and using more teenage words with just a tinge of sass. After a few minutes, she grabbed her blanket and started rolling one of the ties on it, like she had done since her baby days. She wanted to be grown-up, but she still needed the security of her past. I wanted to encourage the blankie behavior, but I knew if I did, it would stunt her moving into her preteens. Each new season is scary for kids; they don't know what to do and aren't sure they will succeed. Knowing the blankie is there while being encouraged to move on is essential. So

TOP TIP #12

As our children continue to grow, we must learn to let them go.

instead of encouraging her to stay young, I took Jasmine shopping for more grown-up clothes, eventually moving on to makeup and other rites of passage that gave her confidence to move into the teen years. While Jasmine was growing up, so was I. I was getting better at letting go.

Following are a few tips the Wolfe Pack learned for handling change.

1. Always foster big dreams in your child.

Encourage your children beyond yourself. We often talked with our cubs about when they moved out and how things would be as they moved on. Make change normal and exciting.

2. Don't make your children feel guilty for growing up.

Yes, they are going off to have some incredible adventures without you, and yes, they will change. Things will never be quite the same again, but you really don't want them to remain the same forever. Get used to change—it never goes away! If their leaving feels like abandonment or rejection of you, then get some prayer from those you can trust to help you in this. Find your strength in God and become strong for them.

3. Never stop dreaming for yourself.

If you feel that your child is going off to some great thing and leaving you behind, then get moving. Your life is not over once your kids are raised—it's just beginning! Your kids will watch you and respect you even more if you keep pressing into great things while they are too.

One of my heroes in life is a doctor I met when I started working in a pediatric intensive care unit. She was in her sixties, had just graduated from medical school, and was a pediatric intensivist. Once her kids had been raised, she had gone back to school to achieve her dream. Now that's a mama who was moving and shaking, and her kids admired her greatly for it.

Don't let change happen just for your children. Make it happen for yourself as well.

4. Reinvent your family times.

What used to work with small kids won't work with college kids. Put effort into continuing to bond and create memories together, even though things might be different now. Our last born is definitely a caboose who loves his brothers. When Austin, his closest sibling, graduated high school, he wasn't as available for family vacations. Instead of seeing it as the end of an era, we packed Sterling up and took him on a special trip to Hawaii to do exactly what he loved (and his siblings not so much): deep-sea fishing. Even though our family looked different now, it was every bit as important and exciting!

Change is good. The next season can seem daunting, but give it time. It just might grow on you! With every new season, reinvent yourself and your family. You will be surprised with each new adventure!

EPILOGUE

THE WOLFE PACK IS STILL NOT DONE!

There you have it: a small peek into how this family navigated the tough things of parenting. Every season brought a fresh batch of challenges and joys. I wish I could share some of the more difficult experiences I mentioned in the first chapter, but perhaps I can another time. Suffice it to say that parenting your little ones into successful adulthood will possibly be your toughest challenge, but with God's help, good books, a great church, strong support systems, and a *lot* of prayer, you, too, can stand on the other side of this parenting journey with a smile on your face.

Parental perfection is not the ultimate goal. Instead, the goal is to produce adult children who are successful in their life work and relationships and who, above all, love God. There isn't a family alive who doesn't have some sort of dysfunction. (Even Adam and Eve had their issues

with sibling rivalry, loss, and rejection.)[55] The hope is that
we can love, forgive our children and ourselves of our
shortcomings, learn better ways of doing this thing called
life, and overcome for the win.

Remember the thirty-seventy split on the responsibility
for the result. Do your part to your best ability. Know that
God cares more about your children than you possibly can!
God knew you and your family before they existed, and He
still chose to give you those children. He has full confidence
in you! Know that in the end, their own choices will rule
the day, so bathe them in prayer, fill them with wisdom, and
entrust the rest to God and the good you have instilled in
them.

The Wolfe Pack started off with glamorous ideals and
lofty aspirations. It would have been quite the glorious story
had it gone as scripted. But if it had, I am not so sure that I
would be writing a parenting book that would benefit you,
the normal parent with normal kids. Instead, I'm afraid you
would feel even more hopeless and discouraged as you faced
challenges that seemed bigger than you. So I think it's a
good thing that those glamorous ideals and lofty aspirations
of ours fell with the sound of a great crashing boom—the
same crashing boom of lamps breaking from pillow fights,
numerous car collisions, and maybe, possibly, a Wolfe cub's
fireworks in a certain porta potty (don't ask me—some
things are better left unsaid!). I wouldn't trade a minute of
those crazy years with little ones, chaos, noise, and mess.

I am grateful that our family wasn't picture perfect.
Our roller coaster ride of child raising had its fair share of
ups and downs and hairpin corners. As we went along, we

found ourselves white-knuckled at times as we held on for dear life. I found so many professionals to help me survive this wild ride; I would have liked to have coffee with them all, but I had to settle for reading their books.

My desire for you is that through some of my stories and thoughts, you can gain courage in your own chaos, find new wisdom and ideas, then throw your arms up in the air with a hoot and a holler of hope and start to enjoy the ride. You will eventually pull into the station and, with the help of all those around you and a huge dose of God's miraculous intervention, your family will all have survived and thrived in some semblance of order.

Parenting is filled with different seasons, and as the Wolfe cubs moved out one by one, I thought I was done. My house stays clean and my refrigerator stays full a lot longer now. Things seemed to have calmed down for the moment, but Cub Number One had her first little one this past summer. Give me a few years and maybe I will add a chapter on grandcubs!

Love every minute of your parenting season, because you don't get any do-overs.

Know that you are not the first parent to enter this stage of life. You are the result of many generations of parents before you, and now you have your opportunity to fashion your arrows to shoot into culture. I like how the following verse calls you, the parent, a warrior. Warriors are very capable and skilled to go for the win. That's you! God loves what you are doing, and He has trusted you with your family. That's a pretty good endorsement!

Like arrows in the hands of a warrior
are children born in one's youth.
Blessed is the man
whose quiver is full of them.
They will not be put to shame
when they contend with their opponents in court.[56]

I am ever so grateful that you have chosen to read this book and strive to be the best you can. Keep up the great work, and let's see what your children become.

ACKNOWLEDGMENTS

I would like to thank everyone who encouraged me to write again after losing five manuscripts to a hard drive disaster. This book (or any other book for that matter) almost didn't happen after those losses, but your words gave me the fuel to press on. So, thank you.

I also owe a huge thanks to my family who gave me all the stories to make this book come alive. Thanks to Lori Baxter, my publishing midwife who helped give birth to my dream, as well as all those at the Scribe Source who worked diligently to get this project completed. Thanks also to Byron Leavitt and Alicia Bilton for their technical and graphic support.

I would also like to say thank you to my New Horizon Church family. Your belief in and love for me are wind in my sails. I am so glad we get to do life together.

A final thank-you to my first nursing instructor who read one of my papers when I was 20 years old and told me I should consider writing a book. I have never forgotten your words.

ABOUT THE AUTHOR

Joel Wolfe is a wife, mother, pastor, and teacher whose passion is to strengthen marriages and families. Born in Guatemala as a missionary's daughter, she is also an RN experienced in pediatric intensive care who brings together her various passions by leading short-term medical, construction, and crusade trips into Africa and Asia. In 2015, she oversaw the building of a maternity clinic on the Uganda–Tanzania border, where women with no previous access to care are now served.

Joel and her husband Dwain have four grown children and have co-pastored New Horizon Church, a vibrant, growing church in Tacoma, Washington, for more than 25 years. Joel loves to read, write, garden, love on her grandson, and travel the world on adventures. Most of all, she lives to glorify God and bring to life His wisdom and knowledge for others.

Join Joel on her website at http://joelwolfe.me, as well as on Facebook at https://www.facebook.com/authorjoelwolfe/ and on Instagram at https://www.instagram.com/authorjoelwolfe/ today!

NOTES

Chapter Two

1. Rom. 8:28 (New American Standard Bible).
2. Fay and Fay, *Love and Logic Magic*, 51.
3. Fay and Fay, 18.
4. Cloud and Townsend, *Boundaries with Kids*, 99.
5. Cloud and Townsend, 18–19.
6. Cloud and Townsend, 134–138.
7. Cloud and Townsend, 60–61.
8. Cloud and Townsend, 61.

Chapter Three

9. Cloud and Townsend, 99.
10. Fay and Fay, *Love and Logic Magic*, 17.
11. Fay and Fay, 94–96.
12. Cloud and Townsend, *Boundaries with Kids*, 18–19.
13. Fay and Fay, *Love and Logic Magic*, 76–77.
14. Fay and Fay, 18.
15. Cloud and Townsend, *Boundaries with Kids*, 135.
16. Cloud and Townsend, 140–141.
17. The Love and Logic website (https://www.loveandlogic.
    com/) has plenty of great ideas for enforceable statements
    as well as great consequences.

18. Fay and Fay, *Love and Logic Magic*, 77–78.

19. Cloud and Townsend, *Boundaries with Kids*, 218–219.

20. *Encourage* means "to infuse you with courage."

21. Fay and Fay, *Love and Logic Magic*, 75.

22. I wish I could take credit for all this great knowledge and truth. I can't. It all came from my author friends. If you want to read more from where I learned all this, look at the Recommended Reading List at the end of this book. The Love and Logic series, for example, offers age-specific books for foundational support as well as some practical ways of dealing with basic situations.

Chapter Four

23. By the way, don't be afraid to read Proverbs to those little sweethearts every day! I can't tell you how many times a particular day's verses were quoted as the day wore on. It felt good to have an ally in Solomon!

24. Num. 23:19 (New Living Translation).

25. Gen. 3:8–13 (New International Version).

26. Gottman, *Raising an Emotionally Intelligent Child*, 101.

27. If you might be a naïve parent like I was, I recommend you get very familiar with scents that are dead giveaways that your kids are up to no good!

28. Cline and Fay, *Parenting with Love and Logic*, 170–172.

Chapter Five

29. Cloud and Townsend, *Boundaries with Kids*, 181–182.

30. Cloud and Townsend, 188–191.

31. Cloud and Townsend, 91–92.

32. Cloud and Townsend, 99.

33. Cloud and Townsend, 99–101.

Chapter Six

34. I used grocery bags for liners, so the kids just pulled them out and relined them. I'm not sure if that was eco-friendly, but it was easy enough!

Chapter Seven

35. Eccles. 10:19 (World English Bible).
36. At the time of this writing, there are various business card companies online where for $20 kids can have 500 cards they design themselves.
37. We found magnets with a peel-and-stick side. We printed his information and stuck it to the magnet. It was very easy and affordable.
38. Scholarships helped as well.

Chapter Eight

39. Gal. 5:22–23.
40. James 3:18.

Chapter Nine

41. Fay and Billings, *From Innocence to Entitlement: A Love and Logic Cure for the Tragedy of Entitlement*, 16.
42. Fay and Billings, 18.
43. Children with social anxiety disorders may need more specific and different approaches. I suggest speaking with a professional for suggestions on how you can be successful in this endeavor.
44. Eph. 4:29, 5:4 (NIV).

Chapter Ten

45. Leman and Bell, *A Chicken's Guide to Talking Turkey with Your Kids about Sex*, 36.

46. Elmore, *Generation iY*, 53–60.
47. See the Recommended Reading List at the end of this book for ideas.
48. Gen. 1:27 (NIV).
49. Sax, *Why Gender Matters*, 13-68.
50. Stanton, "Answering Parents' Questions on Gender Confusion in Children," Focus on the Family, 2009, https://www.focusonthefamily.com/lifechallenges/understanding-homosexuality/gender-confusion-in-children.

Chapter Eleven

51. Cloud and Townsend, *Boundaries with Kids*, 75.
52. Never stop praying for your children. Recently I read the book *Praying Circles Around Your Children* by Mark Batterson. I wish it had been written twenty-five years ago! I would have done everything that book suggests. I heartily recommend that you read it and get inspired.
53. Prov. 22:6 (NIV).

Chapter Twelve

54. Elmore, *Generation iY*, 53–60.

Epilogue

55. Gen. 4.
56. Ps. 127:4–5 (NIV).

RECOMMENDED READING

Arterburn, Stephen, Fred Stoeker, and Mike Yorkey. *Preparing Your Son for Every Man's Battle: Honest Conversations about Sexual Integrity.* Colorado Springs: Waterbrook, 2010.

Batterson, Mark. *Praying Circles around Your Children.* Grand Rapids, MI: Zondervan, 2012.

Cline, Foster, and Jim Fay. *Parenting with Love and Logic: Teaching Children Responsibility.* Colorado Springs: Piñon, 1990.

Cloud, Henry, and John Townsend. *Boundaries in Dating: How Healthy Choices Grow Healthy Relationships.* Grand Rapids, MI: Zondervan, 2000.

———. *Boundaries with Kids: How Healthy Choices Grow Healthy Children.* Grand Rapids, MI: Zondervan, 1998.

Elmore, Tim. *Generation iY: Our Last Chance to Save Their Future.* Atlanta: Poet Gardener, 2010.

Ethridge, Shannon. *Preparing Your Daughter for Every Woman's Battle: Creative Conversations about Sexual and Emotional Integrity*. Colorado Springs: Waterbrook, 2010.

Fay, Jim, and Charles Fay. *Love and Logic Magic for Early Childhood: Practical Parenting from Birth to Six Years*. Golden, CO: Love and Logic Press, 2000.

———. *Love and Logic Magic When Your Kids Leave You Speechless*. Golden, CO: Love and Logic Press, 2000.

Fay, Jim, and Dawn L. Billings. *From Innocence to Entitlement: A Love and Logic Cure for the Tragedy of Entitlement*. Golden, CO: Love and Logic Press, 2005.

Gottman, John, and John DeClaire. *Raising an Emotionally Intelligent Child*. New York: Simon & Schuster, 1997.

Jones, Stan, and Brenna Jones. *God's Design for Sex*. 4 vols. Colorado Springs: NavPress, 2007.

Leman, Kevin. *Have a New Kid by Friday: How to Change Your Child's Attitude, Behavior and Character in 5 Days*. Grand Rapids, MI: Revell, 2012.

———. *Have a New Teenager by Friday: From Mouthy and Moody to Respectful and Responsible in 5 Days*. Grand Rapids, MI: Revell, 2013.

———. *Making Your Child Mind without Losing Yours*. Rev. ed. Grand Rapids, MI: Revell, 2017.

———. *Parenting Your Powerful Child: Bringing an End to the Everyday Battles*. Grand Rapids, MI: Revell, 2013.

————. *Planet Middle School: Helping Your Child through the Peer Pressure, Awkward Moments and Emotional Drama.* Grand Rapids, MI: Revell, 2016.

Leman, Kevin, and Kathy Flores Bell. *A Chicken's Guide to Talking Turkey with Your Kids about Sex.* Grand Rapids, MI: Zondervan, 2004.

McGrath, Alister. *Doubting: Growing through the Uncertainties of Faith.* Downers Grove, IL: InterVarsity, 2006.

Sax, Leonard. *Why Gender Matters.* 2nd ed. New York: Harmony, 2017.

Strobel, Lee. *The Case for a Creator.* Grand Rapids, MI: Zondervan, 2004.

STAY IN TOUCH

Stay in touch with me!

I'm on Facebook and Instagram, and I have my own website to boot. So let's not lose touch! Let's dive deeper into the topics discussed in this book, and together let's explore even more of what God has for us. You can find me at the following places:

Website:

http://joelwolfe.me

Facebook:

https://www.facebook.com/authorjoelwolfe/

Instagram:

https://www.instagram.com/authorjoelwolfe/

Email:

joel@newhc.org

I can't wait to talk with you again soon!

RESTORED LIFE PRESS

Find more incredible books and materials from Restored Life Press. Learn about upcoming projects from compelling, faith-filled authors. Discover life-changing resources and follow along in our revolutionary programs.

UNLOCK YOUR NEW LIFE AT

RESTOREDLIFEPRESS.COM